URBAN ENVIRONMENTS
IN EMERGING ECONOMIES

URBAN ENVIRONMENTS
IN EMERGING ECONOMIES

David L. McKee

HT
384
.D44
M39
1994
West

Westport, Connecticut
London

Library of Congress Cataloging-in-Publication Data

McKee, David L.
    Urban environments in emerging economies / David L. McKee.
       p.   cm.
    Includes bibliographical references and index.
    ISBN 0–275–94938–9 (alk. paper)
    1. Urbanization—Developing countries. 2. Cities and towns—
Developing countries—Growth. 3. Urban ecology—Developing
countries. 4. City planning—Developing countries. 5. Urban
policy—Developing countries. I. Title.
HT384.D44M39 1994
307.76′09172′4—dc20   94–7430

British Library Cataloguing in Publication Data is available.

Library of Congress Catalog Card Number: 94–7430
ISBN: 0–275–94938–9

First published in 1994

Praeger Publishers, 88 Post Road West, Westport, CT 06881
An imprint of Greenwood Publishing Group, Inc.

Printed in the United States of America

The paper used in this book complies with the
Permanent Paper Standard issued by the National
Information Standards Organization (Z39.48–1984).

10 9 8 7 6 5 4 3 2 1

Contents

Preface   vii

I A Preliminary Overview   **1**

1   Some Observations on Physical Structure in Advanced Metropolitan Areas   3

2   Urban Flexibility in Third World Settings   17

3   Dualism, the Rural Exodus, and Urban Expansion   29

II Metropolitan Expansion and Flexibility   **43**

4   Surplus Labor, Squatters, and Urban Structure   45

5   Metropolitan Growth and the Absorption of Urban Places   61

6   Environmental Issues in an Urban Context   73

III Selected Structural Issues   **87**

7   Production for Export and Urban Flexibility   89

8   The Impact of Tourism   103

9   The Urban Role in Small Economies   117

IV Some Policy Perspectives   **131**

10   A General Overview   133

11   Structural and Environmental Imperatives   145

12   Some Final Reflections   157

Bibliography   167

Index   175

Preface

In recent years economists and others concerned with growth and development in Third World settings have devoted considerable attention to urbanization. In some cases that attention has highlighted the city as a receptacle for surplus labor and, presumably, a conduit for the absorption of such surpluses into modern sector activities. This line of reasoning had its roots in the neoclassical synthesis and has produced an elegant body of theoretical material designed to supply logical scenarios concerning the shift in emphasis from rural to urban settings as development proceeds in Third World jurisdictions. No doubt this line of advance owes a considerable debt to the path-breaking work of W. Arthur Lewis (1954).

Another group of development specialists have focused their interests upon Third World cities as catalysts for social change. Their reasoning suggests that the necessities of survival in urban settings break down traditional attitudes, cultures, and ways of doing things in a manner that makes urban residents more amenable to change, thus providing a climate for economic expansion. The work of Bert Hoselitz was an early stimulus for this line of advance (1960).

In the years since Lewis and Hoselitz applied their stimuli, economists and other development specialists have come to regard urban complexes as focal points for the kinds of changes which have been occurring in the Third World. Cities are perceived as sites for modern sector activities, notably manufacturing and services, and thus, as the leaders in the growth of national economies. Literature on the subject is generally aimed at explaining the logic of the urban role and the policy implications surrounding it. Some have suggested that government policy in Third World economies reflects an urban bias and thus is not in the best interests of national development. Others have adopted an even more critical stance, suggesting that in and through cities the system adjusts itself so as to ensure the status quo, which seems to disenfranchise the majority of the population in Third World nations from meaningful participation in expanding modern sector activities.

The present volume will not be aimed at attacking the role that cities are playing in Third World development. The fact that many modern sector activities in Third World economies are urban based is accepted as a given. No attempt will be made to imply that some sort of "trickle-down" mechanism exists whereby growth and/or development spreads from cities to more remote and perhaps less fortunate areas. If economic expansion is to improve the material well-being of the residents of Third World nations, it will probably do so in ways that may well broaden spatial and sectoral imbalances in impacted economies.

The importance of cities in developmental processes appears to be a fait accompli. The function of those concerned with development on a policy level should be to ensure that developmental processes are not impeded. In that regard they may be facing a dichotomy in urban settings. The fact that cities house the leading sectors of most economies sometimes obscures the impact that those leading sectors have on the physical configuring of urban areas. The further fact that the fortunes of components of the modern sector in Third World economies change over time suggests that the fortunes of the cities that house them will change as well. It seems legitimate to ask how urban areas with infrastructures and/or physical forms configured by or for particular economic pursuits can adjust effectively as the needs of such pursuits, or indeed the pursuits themselves, change. How can such urban complexes adjust to meet the changing needs of a changing modern sector, so as to remain an asset rather than a detriment to the processes of change?

The present volume presents the argument that development planners should be concerned about the physical structure of urban places and about the inflexibility of urban forms. It is felt that these issues may easily interfere with economic change and, of course, growth and development. Thus, they deserve the attention of those concerned with development on a national scale, since urban areas are the settings for the bulk of the components of the modern sector.

The argument of the book is presented in four sections. In the first of those, some preliminary concerns are reviewed. To introduce the subject, some observations concerning issues related to physical structure in advanced metropolitan areas are presented. Following that, the discussion turns toward the Third World, where urban flexibility is presented as a development problem. The section concludes with a discussion of dualism, rural to urban migration, and metropolitan expansion.

In the second section, the emphasis switches to the need to provide for physical flexibility in expanding metropolitan areas. In that context, issues relating to surplus labor and urban squatters are discussed. More specifically, it is suggested that the positioning of squatters should be included in the overall plan for the city. Following that, issues relative to metropolitan expansion which absorbs preexisting urban areas are presented. The section concludes with a discussion of environmental issues.

The third section of the book presents a selection of structural issues. First, production for export as it impacts urban settings is presented. Next, an overview of issues relating to tourism in Third World cities is included. Finally, the role played by cities in small economies is considered.

The final section of the book reviews the issues presented earlier, with an eye to emphasizing the need for urban physical planning as a part of any national developmental agenda. It is hoped that the approach taken will assist planners in focusing their energies on various real and potential urban rigidities which, if ignored, may untrack the processes of development.

ACKNOWLEDGMENT

Special thanks are due to Linda Poje, who prepared the typescript and assisted in all phases of manuscript preparation.

Part I

A Preliminary Overview

1

Some Observations on Physical Structure in Advanced Metropolitan Areas

It is no secret that the rise of the modern city can be attributed in large part to the market mechanism. It seems clear that the profit motive provides much of the momentum driving population expansion in the large metropolitan areas of modern nations. Beyond or parallel to profit opportunities, people come to the modern urban complex in search of employment, not to mention to take advantage of modern conveniences (Sundquist, 1970). In another context, it was suggested that the removal of the market mechanism from such agglomerations would cause their economies to grind to a halt (McKee, 1970, 53).

In that same context, it was conceded that there have been cases where completely planned communities have been established. In such cases where private interests are involved, "the market mechanism is directly responsible for their existence" (1970). It was felt that even in cases where such communities were established by the government, they would "still be forced to rely upon the market mechanism to insure their continued success" (1970). The thinking was that the city, in an economy governed by the market mechanism, is dependent upon that mechanism for its continued economic viability. Of course, this view would have to be modified to accommodate the circumstances of urban centers geared to governmental functions and/or nonprofit services.

There appears to be little question that cities, particularly large metropolitan areas, play very important roles in modern economies. It is such agglomerations that provide the climate for the successful continuance of the wide range of economic activities that ensure the ongoing vitality of such economies (McKee, 1991a). By positioning themselves in and around urban areas, economic activities take part in shaping the physical structure of such areas. The urban agglomerations thus configured retain their roles in national economies in proportion to the continuing success of the mix of economic activities that they house.

Unfortunately, the physical configuring of urban areas brings with it certain structural inflexibilities. It is quite possible that an urban environment that was molded to suit the needs of the economic activities which it housed in the past may no longer be suitable to take a strong, ongoing role in the national economy. In such cases the city in question may develop serious economic problems. In other words, inflexibilities in urban structures and capital configurations inherited from the past may seriously damage local economies. Structural rigidities may signal serious sunk costs as well as physical obstacles to growth and change.

In previously robust industrial centers in the United States and other modern economies, problems have emerged in historically strong manufacturing sectors. The problems in question are not simply coextensive with plant closings or competition from newer, presumably more efficient production facilities located elsewhere. By their very existence, closed or abandoned facilities, simply by occupying space, interfere with the efficient operation of the local economy. Their continuing existence ensures that local services must be provided over a wider area than economic efficiency dictates. If new manufacturing ventures are to be added to the urban complex in question, its physical size will be expanded and with it the cost of infrastructure, utilities, and various public services. Clearly, plant closings become problems for physical planners as well as those concerned with shrinking job markets and declining tax revenues.

If the continuing physical presence of fully depreciated and idle industrial sites and/or abandoned or underutilized buildings poses flexibility problems for urban areas, the same can be said for street patterns and other fixed elements in urban infrastructures.

Streets that are too narrow, inadequate parking, and public transit facilities that fail to integrate urban complexes combine to produce additional rigidities which must be dealt with if existing metropolitan configurations are to be expected to retain their operating efficiency and thus sustain roles in the national economy.

No less an observer of the urban scene than Frank Lloyd Wright was quite skeptical of the viability of the twentieth-century metropolis. In a medical analogy, he suggested that "To look at the cross section of any plan of a big city is to look at something like the section of a fibrous tumor" (Wright, 1958, 33). Broadening his analogy, he maintained, "In the light of the space needs of the twentieth century we see there are not only similar inflamed exaggerations of tissue but more and more painfully forced circulation: comparable to high blood pressure in the human system" (33).

As colorful as Wright's analogies may seem, there is little doubt that many major metropolitan areas face problems of congestion and overconcentration. That being the case, various planning procedures and urban renewal schemes may be out of step with actual needs. This may be especially true of practices aimed at rejuvenating the traditional structure of the large city. There is no doubt that such agglomerations play major roles in advanced economies and, indeed, in the international economy as well. Throughout the United States, for example, major metropolitan areas have emerged with functions that impact activities and locations well beyond the regions that house them. Indeed, many newer centers appear to usurp or at least replicate functions or activities that had traditionally been the preserve of a very few of the largest metropolitan areas. The emergence of such centers is partially attributable to growing national and international markets, but beyond the basic demands of such phenomena may be the fact that many activities flourish better beyond the rigidities of older urban environments.

Newer centers may be better equipped to offer potentially profitable settings for activities previously relegated to less efficient positions in older agglomerations. The concentration of industry, commerce, and people seems far less essential today than it may have been in the past. The reduced need for such concentration is largely attributable to advances in transportation and communications. Information can now be made available quickly and cheaply

over long distances, thus precluding the need for various sophisticated or complicated activities to seek the concentration of large
metropolitan areas. New techniques in transportation have made
various locations competitive in securing production facilities
which previously were beyond their reach. "Improvements in
transportation have made it easier to move personnel and materials around, thus reducing the need for centralization" (McKee,
1970, 54).

In recent years, most advanced economies have become service
oriented. That being the case, it should not be surprising that large
cities have become service oriented as well. Traditionally, it may
have been the industrial or manufacturing sector which played a
larger causative role in city size than did service activities. However, the latter appear to have become more influential in determining the physical growth patterns of large metropolitan
complexes in advanced economies. The urban service sector increases in size and complexity as population expands and as the
wealth and sophistication of that population rises. In large metropolitan complexes, service activities were thought to have been
superimposed upon other activities. In other words, such activities
were considered to exist to satisfy the needs of a population which
was present in the area due to job opportunities in other pursuits.
While this perception undoubtedly has historical validity, it over-
simplifies the position that services have assumed in the urban
economy.

Despite the historical significance of manufacturing to urban
expansion, the current importance of services was foreshadowed
in the actual structure of cities. The physical plan of many urban
agglomerations appears to have been constructed around various
services, both public and private. In most cases the commercial
sector, with its cadres of services, occupied the center of the city,
giving rise to the term *central business district* (CBD). Initially, such
centralization was intended to provide all urban residents with
maximum access to the services which cities offered, not to mention the employment opportunities which the offered services
provided.

In the case of retailing and other consumer-oriented services,
developments in transportation have influenced locational patterns within urban complexes. Since motor vehicles have replaced

street railways, consumer habits have been affected by convenience, and retailing functions have pursued residential growth patterns. Such adjustments have seen the rise of neighborhood installations as well as the large shopping centers which have become common in the suburbs of large metropolitan areas.

Certainly, it was the retail sector that was largely responsible for focusing attention on the center of cities. The physical location and structural layout of the urban marketplace influenced the growth of the entire urban area. Congestion in central business districts and the eventual migration of the urban marketplace seem to be at least partially responsible for various structural problems that have emerged in metropolitan complexes in advanced economies. Moves to rejuvenate central city commercial functions in major metropolitan areas notwithstanding, businesses that have remained in downtown areas are facing very strong competition from elsewhere. Of course, any loss of commercial functions from central cities represents a decline in the tax base as well.

Structural problems in the metropolitan complexes of advanced economies are not simply coextensive with what has been outlined above. New suburban expansion brings problems of its own. New suburban commercial and office establishments may not follow traditional urban patterns. Many such facilities can be found lining major approach routes to urban complexes, a circumstance which leads to further traffic congestion. This is especially true where the streets or arteries in question were not built to absorb such traffic.

This type of development further intensifies spread effects as the domestic sector attempts to accommodate itself to expanding commercial facilities. As major suburban thoroughfares become congested with commercial facilities, the land between them becomes less attractive as a residential area. If such a development causes residents to move out, urban spread effects are intensified and the process may well repeat itself indefinitely at ever-increasing distances from the center of the urban complex.

In the United States, spreading urban agglomerations have often been characterized by metropolitan populations that are not increasing as rapidly as the land areas which they encompass (McKee and Smith, 1972). Such expansion has often been accompanied by breached or amended zoning ordinances and building codes, not to mention ill-fated planning procedures. The result is "haphazard or poorly planned community growth" (McKee and Smith, 1972) or, more colloquially, urban sprawl. Where such a configuration develops there is little question that it places serious strictures upon efficient urban expansion.

Few major metropolitan areas in the United States are totally free of inopportune peripheral development. There are many interactive economic and social forces contributing to this phenomenon. When population pressures stemming from urban residential choices which favor suburban over central city locations are added to locational choices of manufacturers seeking open land with access to interstate highway networks, yet needing urban services, the potential for disruptive patterns of urban expansion seems assured. When service establishments catering to the needs of both industry and consumers are added to the mix, further confusion seems inevitable.

Metropolitan peripheries have become the physical locations for ongoing conflicts over spatial needs which involve both secondary and tertiary economic pursuits. Irrespective of the resolution of such conflicts in specific localities, residential patterns are often forced to adjust to the dictates of profit-seeking activities. Most metropolitan complexes are not unified political entities; hence, the problems alluded to above are further complicated by multiple political jurisdictions often lacking coordination between them. Such political fragmentation leads to heterogeneous zoning practice and difficulties with respect to the provision of metropolitan services. Such difficulties may be especially severe in the case of the components of needed infrastructures. Variations in the quality and extent of infrastructure components between segments of the metropolitan mosaic, not to mention variations in the ability and/or willingness of local officials to respond to expanding needs with respect to infrastructures, may arbitrarily direct metropolitan expansion toward specific intrametropolitan jurisdictions and away from others. A clear implication for public policy at the metropolitan level would appear to be the need for cooperation, if not for absolute unity.

It seems almost tautological to suggest that the physical, geographical expansion of metropolitan complexes often brings with it incursions into the efficiency of land use. Often these incursions are obvious, as in cases where the land area encompassed by a metropolitan complex is expanding at the same time that its central core is replete with abandoned industrial and warehousing facilities, not to mention condemned housing and closed-down institutional facilities. The mere fact that such depreciated or abandoned structures exist expands the land area of the metropolitan complex in an increasing cost framework with respect to the provision of social overhead capital, not to mention privately supplied components of the urban infrastructure.

The remedy at the policy level may not be as simple as merely finding new uses for abandoned facilities. Even in cases where condemned or abandoned structures are removed, thus freeing up the land, the stage may not be set automatically for the construction of facilities to house presumably more meaningful (profitable?) activities. The positioning of the now defunct facilities undoubtedly occurred in a manner to utilize the transportation and communication infrastructure of the era which spawned the original enterprises. Those seeking locations for new production facilities may forsake the congestion of traditionally popular industrial areas for locations more accessible to newer transportation facilities. Thus, it would appear that curtailing the overexpansion of the geographical area occupied by metropolitan complexes is more complicated than the mere recycling of land and facilities. By their very nature, cities bring with them structural rigidities which cause the geographical space that they occupy to expand.

The extension of urban space may occur in various ways. One of the more innocuous patterns results from low-density domestic developments characterized by single-family dwellings on relatively large parcels of land. Despite the positive aesthetics associated with such configurations, it could be argued that population densities should be increased in the interests of being able to provide municipal services at reasonable costs (McKee and Smith, 1972).

Urban space can also be extended through the emergence of relatively compact urban configurations which are surrounded by substantial amounts of less-developed or open land. Over time, the open areas may be filled in but the resulting urban mosaic will not necessarily be efficiently integrated. It will certainly not retain the traditional cohesiveness and centrality which were the identifying features of large urban complexes. This lack of cohesiveness may be fueled further by speculation, a form of activity which is often a major driving force in urban expansion.

In advanced economies speculation is the preserve of individual decisions on the part of profit-seeking economic units, each acting independently and/or in competition with each other. Real independent actions of this type, when unencumbered by zoning ordinances, can generate random selections of activities, which may only accidently display any cohesiveness, since they emerged from individual initiatives. Once again confused or poorly integrated or organized patterns of economic activity are put in place, which may hardly contribute to efficient metropolitan development. In place, these activities actually contribute to the rigidities which impair efficient growth patterns.

Of course, physical geography influences urban growth patterns as well. In areas where the terrain is unsuitable for continuous development the effective integration of the metropolitan complex may suffer. Land which is most easily accessible or least in need of refinements will be used first. In this regard, existing transportation facilities combine with terrain in determining expansion patterns. Vehicular routes can produce strip development while rapid transit lines can cause concentrations of business activity at major stations and interchanges. However, it seems to have been the automobile which has had the strongest and most sustained impact on metropolitan expansion patterns. The construction of freeways has caused congestion in certain areas while at the same time influencing both the pace and the direction of expansion.

As suburban areas expand, more public services are required. Perhaps such services can be provided most efficiently on a metropolitan-wide basis. Unfortunately, in most urban complexes political rigidities preclude such service grids. Instead, many services tend to be provided locally by the individual components of the metropolitan complex. Aside from rising tax rates in suburban communities, the situation leads to a heterogeneity of services which is reflected in a poorly integrated metropolitan infrastructure. This may impede economic efficiency and contribute to less-than-optimal metropolitan expansion patterns. Since local infrastructures can influence the location decisions of both businesses and consumers, their impact on growth seems almost self-evident. Some areas will be impacted by growth while others will stagnate. Such a scenario hardly bodes well for those concerned with maintaining the vitality and overall working efficiency of the metropolitan economy.

Expansion that is relatively concentric may be less problematic than that of the ribbon variety. The latter tends to spread urban complexes in a manner which makes the provision of services less efficient. As new businesses emerge along access routes, spread effects are reinforced as suburban arteries become inadequate.

It appears that inflexibilities are built into urban expansion patterns from the outset. This is an irony which can hardly be lost on planners and others concerned with continuing metropolitan viability. The fact that large urban complexes have presented a climate which seems appropriate for business interests has stimulated growth. The success of urban business sites has generated concentration and expansion patterns which seem to create blockages and other inefficiencies. Thus, the success of the urban climate by generating fixed capital facilities, both public and private, simultaneously generates inflexibilities which make ongoing growth and change at best inefficient and at worst hardly feasible. It appears that those concerned with such difficulties should place metropolitan integration and flexibility high on their list of priorities.

The forces at work in advanced economies which have focused attention on major metropolitan areas may have simultaneously signaled the eclipse of various smaller urban centers. The concentration of economic activity in metropolitan complexes coupled with transportation networks linking such complexes with each other, not to mention the world economy, have disenfranchised many smaller urban areas from the mainstream of economic activity in advanced economies (McKee, 1974 and 1975).

The residents of agglomerations which have experienced such a change of fortune may find that they are not receiving a proportionate share of the benefits from economic progress in the national economy. They may live in older housing and work for lower wages (McKee, 1974). By choosing to stay in such locations they themselves become a part of the immobile resource pools which characterize small urban agglomerations which are out of step with the needs of the economy. In cases where such persons own their homes and/or businesses, their plight is often solidified. By being

unable or unwilling to leave such assets behind in favor of presumed opportunities in the mainstream of the economy, they themselves become fixed (immobile) resources or perhaps living
examples of what the rigidities of the urban form can do to economic resources.

Transportation technology appears to be at the root of many of
the structural difficulties facing urban agglomerations in advanced
economies. There is little doubt that the concentrations of economic
activity which emerged at the center of cities and prompted the rise
of large urban populations can be attributed to the railroad. That
form of transportation made major adjustments in outlook and
thus caused adjustments in patterns of social interdependence. It
was seen to be behind the new urban environment, new modes of
work, and even new managerial techniques (McLuhan and Fiore,
1967, 72). Earlier, McLuhan had suggested that the railroad was
even responsible for the abstract grid layouts of American cities, as
well as for what he called the nonorganic separation of production,
consumption, and residence (McLuhan, 1964, 103).

It may have been the railroad which made the development of
very large cities possible and determined their structure to some
extent, but it was the automobile which ultimately changed the
United States from a rural to an urban society. McLuhan and Fiore
termed the automobile the "great leveler of physical space and
social distance" (1967, 8). McLuhan himself saw the automobile as
destroying the human scale of things with respect to both power
and distance (1964, 194). He also accused the automobile of scram-
bling the shape of the industrial town by mixing up the physical
positioning of its functions (103).

Abstracting from McLuhan's colorful methods of description, it
appears as though the automobile has taken over from the railroad
as the organizer behind urban experience. It can be seen as the true
organizer, since physical planners have been cast in a crisis-response mode with respect to keeping circulation functional within
major metropolitan areas. In this regard they must deal not just
with the automobile or the current mode of transportation but also
with the physical positioning of buildings and other capital investments, which have functions to perform in the present economy
while at the same time perhaps presenting rigidities in the face of

changes that may be needed in the normal course of evolution within that economy.

Of course, rigidities in urban structure can and do cause problems in metropolitan areas which are simply growing without major changes in the type of functions they perform or the types of activities they house. In the case of the United States, reality appears to be somewhat more complicated. "While there is widespread recognition that urbanization is undergoing a very fundamental transformation, there is little agreement as to either the major forces at work or the manner in which the urban system is being restructured" (Noyelle and Stanback, 1984, 2). Noyelle and Stanback went on to suggest that the problem lies in focusing on growth itself while at the same time ignoring the underlying processes of change (2). They saw recent changes in urbanization in the United States as being characterized by, among other things, "a widespread transformation of the economic base of cities . . . along with a reorganization of functional linkages that exist among metropolitan centers of the urban system" (2). Behind the changes they cited were "the rapid growth of services, the rise of white collar work, and relative stagnation of production employment" (2).

Noyelle and Stanback saw the changes they cited as largely reflective of responses to forces at work in the economy. Among such forces they listed expanding market sizes, and changes in transportation and technology affecting the production of goods in particular (3). They also included the increasing importance of government and nonprofit activities, especially with regard to the creation of human capital. Last on their list, but very important in the current context, was "the rise of the very large, multiproduct, often multinational, corporation—resulting in the multiplication of locationally distinct service-like corporate establishments: national headquarters, regional sales headquarters, divisional offices, R&D facilities, etc." (3).

In the shift to services envisioned by Noyelle and Stanback, consumer services were considered as playing a relatively minor role (16). Nonetheless, the shift into services has been substantial, and they felt it merits "careful analysis in terms of its probable significance for industrial and employment change within metropolitan economies" (16). They saw the service ascendancy as mainly related to the functioning of producer services as intermediate inputs, as well as to the increasing importance of government and nonprofit services alluded to earlier.

Their analysis was especially significant with respect to the importance of services to urban development. According to them, the very nature of services precluded their being stockpiled. More often than not they could not be shipped and "must be produced to meet the special needs of the customer" (16). In helping with those considerations they saw services production to be disproportionately positioned in metropolitan environments. This positioning they contrasted dramatically with manufacturing, which they perceived to be much more footloose and able "to take advantage of transportation, labor, energy and other economies" (16).

In analyzing the changing economic structure of metropolitan areas in the United States, Noyelle and Stanback have contributed to a basis for understanding the problems of urban physical structure which are more central to the current discussion. For example, if they were correct in downplaying the role of consumer services in the overall service ascendancy, it may well be that the physical positioning of consumer services may have undue impacts upon metropolitan structure. Aside from creating various difficulties alluded to earlier in this discussion, consumer services may on occasion interfere with the location and/or expansion of other service cadres more germane to the ongoing viability of specific metropolitan complexes.

Noyelle and Stanback also appear to be correct in their observations concerning manufacturing. Today most major manufacturing firms are multinational in nature. Historically, manufacturing industries formed the major reason for the growth and continuing viability of certain major cities. Examples abound throughout the developed world. Today such concentrations of firms and/or industries are no longer necessary. Indeed, they may make little economic sense. There is little question that this change in the physical positioning and makeup of manufacturing facilities was made possible through the inputs of various production or business-related services (McKee, 1988).

The freeing of manufacturing endeavors from the necessities of concentration which appear to have prevailed since the industrial revolution has left many traditionally strong manufacturing centers with abandoned plants and damaged economic expectations.

Without getting involved in the deindustrialization debate (Bluestone and Harrison, 1982), suffice it to say that many formerly robust industrial centers find themselves in serious economic difficulties today. Among such problems are those associated with the continuing physical presence of defunct facilities and the infrastructure which serviced them. These examples of sunk capital may mean actual losses in cases where they were not fully depreciated, but even in the absence of such losses they may interfere with efficient growth and change in the metropolitan economy.

As Noyelle and Stanback have indicated, manufacturing activity need not locate in the large metropolitan areas of advanced economies. Indeed, production units need not locate in advanced economies at all. Given this new freedom, it seems clear that future expansion in metropolitan areas will by and large not be brought about by the addition of factory facilities and the infrastructure supportive of such endeavors. It would appear that the continued growth and economic viability of large metropolitan areas will depend more on providing the environment for carrying on the service activities which facilitate production, regardless of where the actual production facilities may be situated. In a word, flexibility in the physical structure of the city may be what will be needed.

2

Urban Flexibility in
Third World Settings

If flexibility is a matter of some significance within metropolitan configurations housed in advanced economies, it would appear to be even more important in the major metropolitan areas of the Third World. Such centers can hardly afford the loss of resources, not to mention viability, which has characterized economic change in the major cities of the modern world. Indeed, such inadequacies where they emerge within Third World cities may well interfere with national development, since most Third World nations look to their major urban centers as the settings to house the leading sectors of their economies. As those leading sectors change, some through growth, others by replacement, their needs change with them. If the metropolitan complexes themselves are unable to provide for such needs, development may be stifled. Thus, it would appear that urban flexibility should be high on the priority lists of those concerned with economic development.

Many factors contribute to the lack of flexibility in Third World metropolitan complexes. In many emerging nations the major urban center is also the seat of government. Many such governmental centers owe their basic structure and positioning to decisions on the part of the imperial powers that once controlled the territories in question. For example, the capitals of various Latin American nations were built in the mountains, away from coastal areas. In Central America the positioning of administrative capitals in the mountains made very good sense at the time when such decisions were made. By locating in the mountains, risks from tropical diseases, flooding, and other unpleasant externalities associated with tropical conditions could be lessened. In addition to the avoidance of natural problems, the sites selected, in theory at least, were much less accessible to the raids of rival imperial powers. Few would debate the rationality of the decision-making process, given the perceived needs of the times. Unfortunately, what may have been quite rational then has left various independent nations with major urban complexes positioned in locations which are hardly optimum with respect to the needs of late twentieth-century development.

One of the circumstances that has made manufacturing facilities geared to world markets viable in Third World economies has been the major improvements in transportation that have occurred during the second half of the twentieth century. Of particular interest are the economics that have been accomplished in ocean transportation. With those improvements, bulky manufactured goods can be shipped long distances at costs that allow them to compete in the major markets of the developed world. Such goods can now be manufactured in various Third World locations, thus permitting the firms in question to avail themselves of large pools of relatively inexpensive labor, not to mention other resources.

In some Third World economies the positioning of major urban complexes and the ad hoc additions to national infrastructures which have evolved from that positioning are not conducive to taking advantage of the transportation improvements alluded to above. The positioning of various Latin American capitals is a major example of this issue.

Problems associated with such positioning appear to be more pressing in smaller nations. Central America is replete with examples of this. The nations in that region are small and, despite their relative proximity to large, well-developed consumer markets, they lack the transportation linkages needed to access those markets in an efficient fashion. Their population centers and thus their urban labor pools are poorly positioned to take advantage of ocean-going transport, and the topography of the region makes ground transportation a poor substitute. Thus, in Central America the positioning of major urban complexes may actually constrain development to some extent. In effect, that positioning has taken away advantages which the nations in question might have been thought to have because of their access to both the Atlantic and the Pacific oceans.

The type of inflexibility alluded to above, whereby the positioning of the major urban center in small nations may impact national development in negative ways, is of course a macroeconomic issue. Indeed, many issues involving major metropolitan complexes in the Third World must be considered to be macroeconomic in scope. If those concerned with economic development at the national level choose to ignore how major metropolitan complexes are impacting their nations, then anything they suggest could be open to question. Although economists and others concerned with economic development have often been accused of having an urban bias, such practitioners can scarcely ignore the macro implications of urbanization in the jurisdictions which concern them.

The way in which urban places and/or urban systems develop can have lasting impacts on the success of the economies which house them. Many smaller jurisdictions may become little more than city-states in the face of urbanization. In larger economies the urban impact may be less obviously overbalanced while still putting its stamp on the direction of development. In economies where one city predominates, the concentration of population and activity can hardly avoid impacting the economic complexion of the entire country. In such jurisdictions accusations of urban bias seem less than surprising. Undoubtedly, the national infrastructure will be geared toward facilitating the operations and, presumably, the expansion of a citified economy. Even in nations where systems of cities have emerged, national economies are influenced strongly by the infrastructure which emerges linking urban places. Thus, it seems clear that the positioning of urban complexes will have strong and unavoidable impacts upon the direction that development can take in Third World jurisdictions.

Attention to this phenomenon on the part of those concerned with public policy should hardly be labeled as evidence of an urban bias. Indeed, sound planning procedures dictate such concern, since urban settings have been identified by economists as the locus of much of the activity of the modern sectors which are recognized as the driving forces in economic expansion.

Evidence that those who have been concerned with the development of national economies have recognized the importance of urban processes can be seen in attempts to determine the physical direction of national development through the positioning of new urban places, or through attempts to influence which existing urban places should grow. In advanced economies such concerns may take the form of alleviating the pressures of continuing expansion in urban complexes which are perceived to be too large. Notable examples of this can be seen in policies directed toward London and Paris earlier in this century (Rodwin, 1970). In the case of London it was hoped that pressure on the metropolis could be alleviated through constructing or encouraging smaller urban places in ways reminiscent of the work of Ebeneezer Howard (Howard, 1946). With respect to Paris the intent was to alleviate continuing population pressure on the capital by encouraging more attention to smaller centers (Hansen, 1968).

The less-than-spectacular results from the policies referred to here are well known. Details concerning them are hardly needed here. If anything, the policy initiatives adopted in the British Isles actually increased the pressure on the London area. If policies directed toward Paris have retarded the growth of that center, such an impact seems less than obvious.

In emerging nations even more ambitious attempts have been made to alter the physical configuration of development through city building. In Latin America efforts have been made to lessen the pressure on existing urban complexes through the construction of new ones. The most celebrated attempt at this occurred in Brazil, where a new national capital was constructed in the interior of that nation. Among the reasons behind such an enterprise were "shifting the face of the country away from the coast, which represents links to the colonial past, toward the geographical center of the country creating a new indigenous urban form; and implanting a growth pole that would accelerate the march to the west" (Katzman, 1977, 42).

The Brazilian experiment may well be a textbook case concerning what city building can achieve with respect to national development. Despite the ground-breaking nature of the experiment and the physically spectacular nature of the new capital, Brazilia, few would suggest that its positioning has altered the physical fulcrum of the national economy. The pressures which generated large concentrations of economic activity and population in Rio, Sao Paulo, and, to a lesser extent, Belo Horizonte are still in place and undiminished, despite the movement of the administrative capital. Certainly, another economic focus has emerged in the Amazon Region, but Brazilia can hardly be labeled as a proximate cause of that. Nor has the Brazilian capital become the gateway of choice for the Amazon Region. The existence of the administrative capital in the interior of the nation has altered the economic nature of the region around it, without dramatically altering the physical positioning of Brazil's sizeable manufacturing sector, not to mention the many private service activities that facilitate it.

Although the positioning of Latin American capitals in colonial times has influenced the direction of development in the nations concerned, this is hardly strong support for experiments like Brazilia. If there are reasons which justify altering the position of capital complexes in Third World settings, those reasons may not have strong economic underpinnings. Where population concentrations are caused by economic considerations, or even where the more viable sectors of national economies revolve around existing urban agglomerations, efforts to change the direction or pace of development through building new cities or moving activities arbitrarily seem fraught with difficulties, since such efforts would appear to be resisting force fields already in place.

Further real-world examples appear to support these contentions. Attempts at capital building on the African continent appear to have had little impact upon development. In Venezuela an attempt to lessen expansionary pressures in Caracas through constructing a new city in a relatively remote site on the Orinoco River had a gestation period replete with difficulties (Rodwin, 1970). Although the city has become functional and has become a factor in the Orinoco Region, there is little evidence that it has been successful in diffusing expansionary pressures in Caracas.

In the Bahamas an attempt at developing an industrial and residential complex on the island of Grand Bahamas has met with limited success (see Thompson, 1979 and Barratt, 1982). Street names, paved roads, and facilities for pleasure craft adorn stands of pine where luxurious residential neighborhoods were to have developed. Some industrial facilities are in place, and a relatively large tourist sector has emerged. Nonetheless, few would suggest that the Freeport/Lucaya area of Grand Bahamas has become a major alternative destination to Nassau for Bahamians seeking an urban setting in preference to more remote locations dependent upon primary activity.

In Third World economies it appears as though urban areas which are already in place tend to house the bulk of modern sector activities which are unconstrained by the needs of the primary sector or the location-specific requirements of the tourist industry. Because of this it should hardly be surprising that economic expansion tends to concentrate in those urban settings. Governments concerned with growth and development may find themselves faced with problems generated by the complexities of urban settings, not the least of which may be a seemingly inopportune positioning of urban complexes as judged by current economic needs. Faced with such difficulties, real-world experiences do not support solutions based upon the construction of new urban complexes, whether as alternative locations of activity designed to alleviate existing pressures or as totally new growth points. A better alternative may be the promotion of continuing viability in existing complexes.

Continuing viability may appear to be an illusive goal in the major metropolitan complexes of the Third World. Many emerging nations do not have the systems of cities that are found in more advanced economies. Hence, if an urban setting is in any way essential to sustained development, major urban configurations become impacted areas. They provide the milieu for expansion, and, by doing so, they seem to ensure that problems relating to sheer size are or will be inevitable.

This line of reasoning is not intended as a launching platform into the debate on the optimum city size or how to attain or retain it. Size presumably measured by population is not the real issue. The problem revolves around the ability of cities to retain their viability as centers of economic strength as change occurs. Size (population?) becomes an issue in that regard if it stifles economic activity and prevents change. Problems of that nature can occur in relatively small urban agglomerations if the infrastructures that service them become insufficient, and especially if those infrastructures cannot be altered to meet changing and/or expanding needs. Hence, the main problem is not size per se but rather flexibility. Certainly, an increasing population can complicate the situation, but to suggest that population is the root of the problem by itself is probably an oversimplification.

Economists have long been concerned with the role that urbanization has assumed in the processes of growth and change. Implicit in the work of W. Arthur Lewis on the movement of surplus labor into Third World metropolitan areas (Lewis, 1954) is the idea that such centers are "the location of modern sector activity and thus . . . pressure points with respect to growth" (McKee, 1991a, 18). There is little doubt that the profit-seeking activities of the modern sectors of Third World economies tend to concentrate in major urban areas. It has been suggested that such concentrations are occurring because urban settings provide a favorable climate in a Schumpeterian sense (McKee, 1991a). If cities can be considered as the focal points for growth and change in a Schumpeterian sense, it is hardly surprising that those concerned with economic expansion in Third World settings are showing a continuing interest in them.

In a Schumpeterian vein a system of thought known as "pole theory" has emerged which addresses the ways in which leading economic activities determine the direction of growth. In its initial form, pole theory was hardly intended as an explanation for the growth of cities. Yet it is hardly surprising that in the hands of some it has taken on an urban slant. In an often-quoted passage, François Perroux, who is regarded by many to have been the originator of pole theory, declared that "growth does not appear everywhere at the same time, it becomes manifest at points or poles of growth, with variable intensity, it spreads through different channels, with variable terminal effects in the whole of the economy" (1970, 94).

It is hardly an extravagant reach for some to have placed a spatial connotation on the concept of the growth pole, although Perroux's idea of space was much more complicated than mere physical positioning (Perroux, 1950). For the present it will suffice to supply a hybrid view of the growth pole concept adequate to illustrate its urban context. Growth poles have been described as "leading industrial sectors in terms of size and/or impact" (McKee,

1991a, 87). If such activities are generally attracted to urban areas it seems safe to assume that such locations have a major involvement in the processes of growth and change. As growth poles or leading sectors are replaced over time as an integral part of change itself, the complexion (climate) of the urban area concerned must adjust to the needs of new and changing growth poles. Failure to do so would result in the economic eclipse of the urban area concerned.

The identification of specific cities as the potential location of a series of growth poles or leading economic sectors through time is an oversimplification of what cities do. Nonetheless, it does serve to reemphasize the need for flexibility in urban configurations. It may not be realistic to assume that a particular city can continue to host serially successive leading economic activities. Indeed, it may not be necessary that it do so. What does appear to be essential is that it require some type of replacement activity should existing pursuits fall into decline. Many historically strong manufacturing centers in advanced economies are testimony to such needs. In other words, despite the fact that cities appear to provide the climate for various economic activities, there is no guarantee that specific centers will continue to prosper simply because they exist.

In the Third World the economic circumstances of specific urban areas may be even more tenuous, despite the fact that they harbor the nonprimary activities of the modern sector. Advances in transportation and communications have brought many Third World jurisdictions into the world economy in ways that were previously all but impossible. Multinational firms are locating production facilities in Third World settings with an eye to supplying their international customers. Thus, the emergence of production facilities is no longer constrained by the needs of the local market. Although import substitution and/or the expansion of domestic market potential still facilitate or encourage the establishment of production facilities, manufacturing for export in facilities controlled by multinational firms is very much a part of the industrial landscape in many emerging nations. Such production facilities tend to be located in urban areas, the major provisos being that the areas in question have the appropriate infrastructure to ensure international linkage and, of course, a suitable labor pool and local business environment.

Urban areas that are suitably situated and endowed may make major contributions to domestic expansion through hosting elements of business organizations which are part of the international economy. Of course, to the extent that the business organizations are at risk from economic crises beyond the boundaries of the jurisdictions hosting specific facilities, the overspill from such crises may find its way into those jurisdictions. The severity of such effects will depend upon the position of the impacted facilities with respect to their host economy. Certainly, the impact can be serious in urban areas where the export-oriented facilities are major players in the local economy.

Production cutbacks, layoffs, and plant closings can interfere with the development aims of Third World nations. In cases where such negative adjustments are permanent, urban areas can be left with infrastructure components which are redundant if the closed or vacated facilities are not taken over by new activities. This type of problem has a familiar ring in advanced nations where entire regions have been impacted; witness, for instance, the plight of what has been characterized as the rust belt in the United States. In that region the phenomenon has been characterized as deindustrialization (Bluestone and Harrison, 1982). Without entering the debate with respect to the utility of that concept as applied to advanced economies, suffice it to say that plant closings and layoffs may be even more devastating when they occur in Third World settings, since those locations may have fewer and less robust adjustment options.

Once again flexibility emerges as a major issue. If development in Third World economies is being driven by the success of foreign manufacturing facilities then events beyond the control of domestic policymakers may threaten that development. Cities which house the manufacturing operations in question may find themselves with redundant or inflexible infrastructures, should the operations shut down. They may be faced with larger expenses to alter infrastructures in order to attract replacement industries. Even vacated industrial facilities may become a part of the general flexibility issue, if they are not recyclable.

To date, the discussion concerning industrial change has revolved around the implications of retrenchment involving the operating units of multinational enterprise. Such adjustment problems may appear all the more severe since they seem to involve economic sovereignty and appear to signal a certain amount of impotence or helplessness on the part of the nations concerned. Unfortunately, the negative overspills from economic change cannot be attributed solely to the circumstances described above. Change under the best of circumstances is a painful process, and change appears to be central to profit-seeking economies, whether international or domestic (McKee, 1991a).

Urban places in the Third World, by virtue of the fact that they do harbor many of the activities of the modern sectors of national economies, must expect to be faced with continuous change. Indeed, economic success (growth?) must be expected to occur at the expense of certain economic activities and in favor of others. For sustained development to be achieved, Third World economies must find ways in which economic expansion can occur against the backdrop of the rising and falling fortunes of individual firms and industries. In their urban settings the rise or fall of specific firms or industries present serious flexibility constraints which the urban places concerned must master if they are to continue to provide the climate for economic expansion.

In many urban settings in the Third World this scenario is further complicated by a continuing influx of population. Certainly, rising populations add to the problems of flexibility already cited, but it must be reemphasized that flexibility is rarely a mere function of population absorption. This perception is no doubt a spin-off from the considerable body of work which was initiated by the contribution of W. Arthur Lewis, referred to earlier in this chapter. Despite the undisputed quality of this line of reasoning, it may not be helpful to conclude from it that growth problems in Third World metropolitan complexes result from inadequate absorptive capacities in the modern sector, coupled with continuing population pressure from displaced rural workers. Aspects of the urban surplus labor issue will be dealt with later in the present volume. To insert them here might detract from the macroeconomic focus of the present discussion, namely, the impact of metropolitan complexes on national economies.

There is little doubt that the developmental aspirations of Third World nations must depend upon the emergence of a viable and growing assemblage of business activities which can sustain an expansionist climate. To do so, it is hardly necessary to attract components of the leading sectors of the world economy and to replace those on a continuing basis with components of new world leading activities as they emerge. If certain Third World nations do indeed host such activities, they may not necessarily have their developmental ambitions blunted merely because the activities in question are replaced or bested as leaders (growth poles?) in the world economy. What matters to Third World host nations is that the activities in question continue as economically viable units capable of positive domestic impacts. Since the settings for most such enterprises tend to be urban, those concerned with development must involve themselves in ensuring that the urban infrastructure continues to be adequate to meet the needs of the industrial units which they host. If those needs change, the issue appears to be once again one of flexibility.

Economists have recognized for some time that activities need not be of the leading sector variety to sustain ongoing positive impacts. This is the trickle-down effect posited by Albert O. Hirshman (1958). It is quite possible that production units which have been positioned in Third World settings to avail themselves of a less costly environment may make continuing positive impacts upon the economies which host them. If they provide jobs and outlets for underutilized resources, they can contribute to an improving economic climate and to the growth of modern sector activities, both of which are essential if sustained economic improvements are to be the result. It seems inevitable that positive impacts from such activities will put more pressure on the urban complexes that house them. Once again urban areas will have macro impacts which must concern those employed in development planning on a national scale, accusations of urban bias notwithstanding.

Of course, export-oriented activities would appear to have more immediate prospects for expanding the modern sectors of Third World economies than would activities aimed at domestic markets. In smaller Third World jurisdictions there may be little immediate potential for developing products for domestic markets. Even in larger nations the development of domestic markets is constrained by the percentage of the population associated with the modern sectors of the economies in question. Thus, domestic market expansion returns the focus of the development problem to labor absorption, most probably in an urban setting. Domestic markets cannot expand unless those on the demand side have the funds to avail themselves of what is offered. The symbiosis between foreign and domestic markets, and hence development, seems clear. Accessing foreign markets makes income available to consumers and thus encourages the expansion of domestic markets accompanied once again by needed labor absorption.

It seems clear that production for export has advantages to Third World nations in spite of potential difficulties with economic sovereignty. These advantages are even more basic than the obvious benefits from earning needed foreign exchange credits, a subject well beyond the scope of the current discussion. The risks cited earlier include potential difficulties in the international economy and, of course, problems of factor immobility and inflexibility associated with the changing fortunes of foreign-oriented operations.

Both export-oriented and domestic production tend to be carried out in urban settings. For the national economy to retain its viability and thus expand, the urban settings must be capable of efficient physical expansion and adjustment. Because of this it seems clear that urban areas cannot be left to their own devices by those concerned with national development. Such practitioners must hold an ongoing concern for the adequacy of urban infrastructures and for the transportation and communication facilities needed to ensure a continuing role for activities housed in their urban areas. It would appear that, rather than trying to alleviate real or imagined urban congestion (overconcentration?) by the construction of new urban places, it may be more advisable to put the effort into improving the efficiency of those that exist. The search for urban efficiency and flexibility in Third World settings is very much a macroeconomic issue. Of course, there are many issues internal to the economies of urban places, and a selection of those which may untrack the macro role of the city in Third World economies will be the subject of ensuing chapters of this book.

3

Dualism, the Rural Exodus, and Urban Expansion

Since urbanization appears to play such an important role in economic development, it is surprising that more attention has not been paid to urban structure and the rigidities that form imposes on the direction and extent of growth. It seems almost tautological to say that urbanization causes economic activity to concentrate in specific locations and is thus one of the major causes of regional disparities in material welfare and growth potential. At one time it was thought that such disparities were negative elements in the expansion process, which might have to be overcome on the road to economic improvement (McKee and Leahy, 1974).

Disparities caused by urbanization may even be at the root of accusations of urban bias which are sometimes leveled at economists in textbook treatments of Third World development (e.g., Todaro, 1989). If urban concentrations of economic activity have attracted the attention of policymakers, who have adjusted their priorities to supply improvements in infrastructures and other forms of social overhead capital to meet the needs of those activities, this may well be considered as urban bias in some circles. Those circles would include all who have subscribed to the normative judgment that part of the development process, as encouraged by government, should be the elimination of disparities in welfare levels and, presumably, growth potential across the map. Such a goal might be thought to be difficult if not impossible to achieve in the face of adjustments in government priorities occasioned by efforts to meet urban needs; thus, the accusation of bias.

Those who accuse economists and development planners of urban bias may be a subset of a declining cohort of practitioners who still adhere to the belief that balanced growth is both desirable and capable of being attained. The prevailing majority opinion among economists appears to concede that imbalances are inevitable in economies based on private enterprise. In this century, subscribers to that opinion have included Joseph Schumpeter and Gunnar Myrdal, adherents to widely disparate ideological positions. There are differences among economists with respect to how to deal with negative externalities which result from disparities. Those differences are well beyond the context of the current discussion. As has been stated earlier (Preface), the main thrust of this book has to do with various structural and environmental difficulties associated with urbanization, any or all of which may be capable of untracking, or at least impeding the development of Third World economies.

The development of an economy that is urban based is dependent upon adjustments in agriculture and/or the supply of food, which frees labor to follow the new urban pursuits. This requires not only that agriculture should become more efficient but that it should address the problem of supplying the food needs of the population, both urban and rural. Failure in this regard will make the emerging urban emphasis a costly one dependent upon food imports. Even a successful agricultural adjustment is no guarantee that economic growth will be achieved. "Urbanization is a necessary but by no means a sufficient condition for economic development" (McKee and Leahy, 1974). It may be essential for the emergence of a sophisticated economy, but it can bring with it various rigidities that can untrack or impede expansionary processes.

It has long been recognized that cities have evolved as integral components of the machinery of production and distribution (Ratcliff, 1949, 20–21). In spite of this, and in spite of the fact that advanced economies appear to require urban environments, those very environments can block adjustments in the urban activity mix simply because they emerged to facilitate earlier needs. By the very fact that urban places are successful in hosting specific economic pursuits which are profitable and expanding, they will attract population and will grow themselves. In the case of Third World metropolitan areas there is little reason to assume that there is a direct relation between population influx and the expansion of the seemingly successful economic pursuits. Indeed, there may not even be strong reasons to assume that specific successful pursuits will remain as such or that urban areas housing them will continue to grow and prosper in an economically efficient manner. Clearly, urban planning with emphasis on flexibility appears to be desirable, if Third World cities are to be successful as focal points for ongoing economic expansion.

The linking of urbanization and economic development is by no means a new idea. The growth of population in urban and industrial areas was seen by Bert Hoselitz as an inevitable consequence of economic expansion (1960, 159). Hoselitz was curious as to what extent an urban culture can be considered to be a catalyst for the values and beliefs of people in ways that might encourage expansion. Most assuredly, the stronger elements in an economy are generally positioned at or near urban centers. Less satisfactory development is to be found in more remote areas.

As was suggested by Gunnar Myrdal, the play of market forces causes the bulk of successful economic activity to be grouped in certain locations. Myrdal saw this reality to be a self-reinforcing, increasing function of the poverty of the economy in question (1957, 26–42). If Myrdal was correct, large urban agglomerations might be a logical consequence of the circumstances facing Third World nations. Further support for this contention can be found in the work of Bela Balassa, who suggested that poorly functioning price systems and inadequate infrastructures combine to encourage significant "agglomerative tendencies" (1965, 23).

It seems as though the agglomerative tendencies alluded to above will undoubtedly exaggerate the spatial imbalances which can be expected in economies driven by the profit motive. Of course, imbalances are inevitable in profit-seeking economies and public policy initiatives aimed at them directly may not be indicated, unless, of course, they can be shown to be impeding economic progress and with it the potential of the economy for improving the material welfare of the population.

One way in which the imbalances in question may be impeding material progress is through an implicit support of dualism—a phenomenon whereby two economic and/or social systems exist within the same nation. Typically, in the case of economic dualism, the two systems in question are at different levels of strength or sophistication. In cases where a modern economy is superimposed upon a more traditional one, the former may be located in and around urban areas. Since one aspect of dualism is the inability of the two economies to relate to each other or form linkages, the situation as it has been described may impede progress. In fact, the urban settings of the modern economy may draw resources away from rural areas, thus increasing disparities in material circumstances and rendering the dual nature of the economy in question more evident.

The emergence of such circumstances will do little to dispel the suspicions of urban bias referred to earlier. Without returning to that debate and without joining the fray concerning whether or not dualism itself is a useful concept (see Santos, 1979), it can be said that successful, profit-motivated activities, when located in urban areas, draw resources, particularly ambitious people, from rural areas. This by definition causes the urban areas in question to become larger. Whether they become stronger is a complicated issue which requires an understanding of what happens to incoming populations and how that impacts the urban economy.

Postponing the labor absorption issues for the moment, it can be said that as urban populations expand, ever-increasing demands for social overhead capital emerge, as do pressures on the urban infrastructure. Of course, these increased pressures and demands, if they cannot be met, may contribute to urban inflexibilities, which in turn may damage the efficiency of the urban economy, or, more specifically, its leading profit-seeking components.

Once again, labor and welfare issues aside for the moment, it would appear that serious attention to urban planning is indicated if urban agglomerations in the Third World are to retain the flexibility which they will need to maintain their role of host for expanding modern sector activity. A climate conducive to growth requires not only that the needs of current businesses are met, but that the emerging needs of new players on the economic scene are met as well. Aside from the specifics of what may be needed in individual cases and settings, the most general need must be for flexibility. Planners must encourage urban environments which are not static, but which change with the needs of their components. Given the inflexibilities of capital, both public and private, what seems to be indicated is a very tall order, even with careful planning. The debacles which have occurred in Third World settings where planning has been neglected are far too obvious. What seems to be less obvious is any general movement toward the types of planning and control procedures which appear to be indicated.

The seeming neglect of urban planning needs in the Third World may not be too surprising against a backdrop of neoclassical explanations of how change occurs. Earlier in this chapter it was suggested that population movements which contribute to urban population growth presume improvements in agriculture which free workers from the soil. C.A. Tisdell pointed to the fact that classical economic thinking suggests a continuing surplus labor pool in the rural areas of the Third World (1990, 117–118). Thus, there is always a virtually unlimited supply of workers who are available, in theory at least, to join in modern sector activities.

Since most modern sector activities are housed in urban settings, surplus rural labor must migrate, if it is to be absorbed into modern sector pursuits. Certainly, rural-to-urban migration is increasing, but "In the urban environment the matter of labor absorption becomes critical very quickly, since new arrivals have few skills to offer to prospective employers" (McKee, 1988, 27). The problem does not end with the lack of jobs. Not only is labor absorption far from the automatic process that neoclassical thinkers have presumed it to be, but beyond that, "few city governments in the developing world are able to cope with such rapid urban growth, and as a result essential infrastructure is often inadequate, and the unhealthy environments that have developed have become a source of disease and international concern" (Tisdell, 1990, 117, referring to World Commission on Environment and Development).

Despite such problems, it appears as though the processes of economic development and urbanization are inextricably linked. Unfortunately, the actual processes of growth and change in Third World metropolitan areas have received surprisingly little attention. "Cities grow in size as a natural consequence of improvements in agriculture and the expansion of industry" (McKee and Leahy, 1974). It has been suggested that dual labor markets exist in the urban areas of the Third World "not just between agriculture and manufacturing" (Tisdell, 1990, 125).

This duality in urban labor markets may have the potential for impeding development. Whether such an impediment is strictly local in nature or wider in scope depends upon how it impacts the needs of the modern sector and how government priorities must be adjusted to deal with the negative externalities of dualism in an urban setting. Neoclassical thinking implies that as surplus labor enters the urban employment market, it must be absorbed if ongoing economic progress is to be achieved. Unfortunately, many fledgling urbanites lack the skills needed to function in their new environment; thus, their arrival "merely relocates the surplus labor problem in a setting which makes it more difficult to control" (McKee and Leahy, 1974). When natural increases in urban populations are considered along with in-migration, the labor absorption issue takes on even more serious proportions.

The emergence of dualism in urban labor markets implies inadequate absorptive capabilities in the modern sector and, as a consequence, an impairment of overall development potential. Labor absorption in Third World metropolitan areas may be an automatic process as implied by neoclassical thinkers, but it may not be capable of the throughput necessary to keep rural and urban real wages in balance. If such a balance is effectuated, it may be external to modern sector activities in urban settings. As Tisdell suggests, "Outlets for small-scale self-employment and casual employment in urban areas co-exist with more formal possibilities for employment" (1990, 125). Whether knowledge of such opportunities exists or not, "the flow of migrants continues, based upon unrealistic expectations, worsening survival capabilities in rural areas, or noneconomic considerations" (McKee, 1988, 28).

The continuing flow acts as a depressant on wages in the most menial urban occupations (McKee, 1988, 29). Indeed, it was suggested earlier that "A continual influx of people drawn to the city by over-optimistic expectations with respect to opportunities for advancement may ultimately depress urban income levels below what they are in rural areas" (McKee and Leahy, 1974). This line of reasoning hardly impeaches the body of theoretical analysis initiated with the work of W. Arthur Lewis (1954). Lewis, in his analysis, saw real wages in both rural and urban areas equating at subsistence levels, where they might remain indefinitely due to continuing oversupply in labor markets.

As bad as the scenario put forward by Lewis may seem, reality may be even more complicated. There may be little room in modern sector activities in Third World metropolitan areas to accommodate the continuing flow of new migrants at any price. Thus, the survival of such new arrivals has little to do with wages in the modern sector, where they are unemployable due to a lack of basic skills. Given such circumstances, the emergence of dualism in urban settings hardly seems surprising. It has been suggested that many solve their survival problems by actually reconstructing their rural environments in urban settings, a practice that may well represent a direct interference with the urban economy (McKee and Leahy, 1974).

New entrants who are not absorbed into the modern sector are finding methods of survival exterior to it. This can mean an urban peasant existence based on barter or some form of self-employment which generates income. Some development specialists might characterize the existence of such life-styles as evidence of dualism. Of course, a dualism of this sort may imply a long-range, if not permanent, continuation of two very different types of urban economy. Difficulties with respect to the efficient expansion of Third World metropolitan areas appear to be unavoidable under this scenario. This is so because both the modern economy and that based upon an urban underclass are presumed to be growing in the same geographical area. Such circumstances can hardly render the tasks of urban planners more manageable.

To development specialists embracing neoclassical economic thinking, dualism may represent a serious blockage in the way of economic growth. Having cut their teeth on the analysis of automatic economic processes in advanced nations, they see material betterment in Third World locations as a function of the successful expansion of the profit-seeking activities of the modern sectors of the economies in question. The bulk of modern sector activities is perceived to be urban based, and such practitioners would be critical of circumstances which might impede the efficient expansion of those activities. If dualism in an urban setting should impede efficiency with respect to the operation of the modern sector, it would be viewed with alarm; if not, it would be ignored.

Other students of development, who are concerned with the urban setting, are less willing to acknowledge urban underclasses as divorced from the urban mainstream. Bryan Roberts has suggested that the "issue of the coexistence of wealth and poverty, modernity and traditionalism in cities of underdeveloped countries," which he labels as "apparent paradoxes," can frequently "be explained in terms of the way in which capitalism has expanded in underdeveloped countries" (Roberts, 1978, 109). To support such a position he recognized the necessity of showing "that the traditional activities of low productivity carried out by the urban poor are linked to, and affected by, contemporary industrialization and by the consumer preferences this industrialization has engendered" (109). Alternatively, Roberts suggested that one could argue that urban poverty stems from overurbanization whereby subsistence activities are transferred to an urban setting (109). It may be recalled that such a transference of a subsistence way of life was alluded to earlier in the current discussion, but not in the context of the overexpansion of Third World metropolitan areas. The point at issue was the movement of subsistence activities as a means of survival.

Although survival in dualistic circumstances appears more attainable in urban rather than rural settings, Roberts feels that an erosion of the independence of the poorer of the two urban economies is inevitable. He bases his argument on the presumption that urban settings cause the consumption of even the poorest residents to become dependent upon the market (112). In support of his position he points out that even the poor tend to incur transportation expenses in getting to work and that foodstuffs purchased in local markets may be produced on profit-oriented farms rather than by peasants (112–113). Beyond that, Roberts points to a widening use of canned and/or processed foods. "Other costs, such as educational and health expenses, begin to figure in the budgets of low-income families; amusements such as cinemas, sports and gambling become part of family budgets" (113). Thus, he suggests that the budgets of the poor are likely to include ever-larger outlays on goods and services originating in the modern sector.

As Roberts has stated the case, it would appear that the integration of the poorer elements of the urban population into the modern economy is not occurring in a positive way. They are merely becoming increasingly dependent upon that economy while not necessarily gaining many real benefits from it. In further support of his position Roberts suggests that "the self employed worker or small, family enterprise is often dependent on merchants or large scale enterprises who provide the capital or materials" (116). In what appears to be almost an urban version of the putting out system, "These large-scale operators sell the product of their own shops or use it to complement their own production, as when a shoe factory commissions out-workers to trim shoe leather" (116).

Although Roberts perceived the relationship between the poor and more fortunate segments of metropolitan populations in rather negative terms, there are others who see the position of the poor in a more positive light. Granted that immediate absorption into relatively well-paying modern sector pursuits is beyond reasonable expectations for most in-migrants from the countryside, and that the types of exploitation alluded to by Roberts may be reasonably common, the urban setting may afford a better survival potential for those adopting it. "Whether participation in the informal sector is a way station on the road to a better existence or a life membership in an urban underclass remains to be seen" (McKee, 1988, 29).

Alejandro Portes and Lauren Benton suggested that the informal sector in urban settings provides a pool of labor that is sometimes utilized by employers in ways that do not afford workers the advantages of a formal wage contract (1984, 589–613). Comparisons of such circumstances with established practices in developed economies may be less than helpful. Despite real drawbacks, the experience, not to mention the pay, however small, which workers gain may actually improve their long-run prospects while securing their short-run survival. "[T]he existence of the informal sector in the urban environment . . . acts as an attraction to would-be rural emigrants, since as a 'halfway house,' it provides prospects of some income while waiting for employment in the formal urban sector" (Tisdell, 1990, 126).

Despite the fact that urban settings are recognized by those adopting them as more survivable than rural alternatives, a continuing influx of such populations to Third World metropolitan areas may cause serious problems for economic expansion. "Growth in the urban economy would take place more quickly if the surplus labor were left in the rural areas" (McKee and Leahy, 1974). Indeed, Todaro has suggested that migration to cities should be restricted (1971). Of course, such suggestions imply a recognition of the problem potential of a continuing influx of surplus labor. For impacted metropolitan areas the problems surpass the issue of labor absorption. As the urban population expands, additional demands are placed upon the local economy for social overhead capital. Such demands may force the alteration of government priorities in ways that impede the emergence of an infrastructure suitable for economic expansion. Thus, rising populations introduce inflexibilities which can curtail economic growth.

Beyond that, rising populations can actually shape the dimensions and physical characteristics of metropolitan complexes. By doing so they can seriously damage the efficiency of the local economy. In cases where this occurs, the impacted metropolitan areas may have their long-range potential for labor absorption impaired. Indeed, negative externalities may be felt well beyond urban boundaries. Since the metropolitan areas in question are recognized as housing the stronger elements of national economies, damage to their operating efficiency can also damage the national economy and its growth potential.

Despite the arguments against the continuing expansion of metropolitan populations based upon efficiency, human perceptions concerning economic opportunities or, at the very least, survival options are fueling a continuing urban influx throughout the Third World. Aside from expectations on the part of potential migrants concerning better opportunities in urban settings, events beyond the boundaries of metropolitan complexes are also serving as stimulants to migration. Anecdotal evidence from specific localities in Mexico illustrates this point. There, local employment options beyond the metropolis have diminished (Arizpe, 1982, 26).

When Arthur Lewis posited the existence of a continuing labor surplus in the rural areas of the Third World, many were quick to follow his lead in examining the growth options dependent upon labor absorption in the modern sectors of metropolitan economies. On the policy level, some, including the present author (McKee and

Leahy, 1974), recommended slowing the flow of migrants into metropolitan areas by creating employment options in rural areas. "Why not encourage cottage industry and small-scale labor-intensive enterprise in rural areas" (1974). The argument was that such a practice would provide a certain amount of training while introducing rural people to the market economy. Of course, the policy, if successful on an adequate scale, would hold back premature movements of population into urban areas.

On the surface, restraining the rural exodus seems like a reasonable and even important policy initiative. If successful it would not only give besieged metropolitan areas breathing time, but it would also make a positive contribution to the national economy. Unfortunately, policies can be logically sound in theory and even commendable normatively, while at the same time being unworkable. Stanching the rural to urban flow in Third World settings may fit this description. Indeed, the problems of growing urban populations could not be solved by merely stanching the flow. Natural increases of substantial proportions would still have to be reckoned with.

The linkages between rural labor surpluses, burgeoning metropolitan populations, and economic expansion at the national level can be better understood against a backdrop depicting causal elements behind the rural exodus. On a superficial level it is easy to begin by saying that improved agricultural methods create labor surpluses which are then free to migrate. There is no doubt that the mechanization of agriculture displaces workers. So does land fragmentation among peasant holdings, which is a widespread problem in Third World economies. So does the repossession of land worked by peasants in order to expand the cultivation of commercial export crops, a practice which has been occurring in Central America. The same result occurs when fertile land is exhausted by overcropping or through erosion, as has been the case in Haiti. It seems obvious that there are many scenarios other than economic efficiency which produce surplus labor in agricultural settings.

It seems obvious that all of the scenarios referred to in the preceding paragraph may add to the migratory stream. Beyond those, people migrate to escape the attention of village moneylenders, or unacceptable family circumstances, or simply because the urban environment appears to offer greater opportunities. For such migrants it is doubtful that the creation of nonagricultural employment in rural areas would have held them in place. In some areas, many parts of the Caribbean for example, field work and even peasant life-styles are viewed to be demeaning. Thus, those who can move into urban settings.

Ironically, in Third World economies where components of developmental infrastructures are being extended beyond major cities, employment opportunities in newly reached areas can as easily be destroyed as created in the process, and new transportation and communications facilities may make the city more accessible, thus creating a further stimulus to migration. In such circumstances, those who may have been introduced to the money economy through cottage industry may be encouraged to advance their ambitions in urban settings. In some cases rural profit opportunities are destroyed by better access to the city. Artisans and small rural producers cannot compete with urban merchandise.

Arizpe recounts examples of urban impact in Mexico. With better access "Traditional occupations begin to disappear" (1982, 27). She went on to explain the disappearance of the local folk-doctor and midwife. "People no longer hire the village fiddler or guitar player" (27). "The firecracker-maker, the altar-decorator, the teachers of traditional dances, the medicine woman, the tile-roofer, and the prayer man, have all lost their jobs" (27). Although the evidence put forward by Arizpe is local in nature, it seems clear that such occurrences are possible in other settings where economic change is in evidence. Arizpe goes on to explain that "Small local business and itinerant trading have also declined . . . taken over by the large commercial enterprises in the regional cities and the monopolistic activities of merchants from the central market La Merced in Mexico City" (27).

Arizpe suggests that what she has been describing has "been destroying the means by which peasant families had once been able to obtain cash" (27). To make matters worse, she explains that the cash needs of such families are on the rise. Electricity, more frequent bus trips, and in one setting alluded to "drinking and irrigation water, are all new services that must be paid for" (27).

The message seems clear that even in rural settings a better integration with the urban economy destroys old ways of livelihood while making new services and perhaps opportunities available. Discussions revolving around accusations of urban bias or even suggestions involving cutting the flow of rural to urban migration seem strangely antique. With no resounding cheers for Third World metropolitan areas, they must be recognized for what they have become. If they are indeed the fulcrum of economic change, then they must be planned so that change can be facilitated. To date, planning, with few exceptions, if it exists at all, is cast in the familiar crisis response mold. Such procedures are having little impact and must be replaced by planning for flexibility with an eye to facilitating change. Only thus can this often unwilling vehicle for change, the Third World metropolitan area, be kept in motion.

Part II

Metropolitan Expansion and Flexibility

4

Surplus Labor, Squatters, and Urban Structure

As has been emphasized earlier in this volume the continuing movement of population into Third World metropolitan areas can create problems which impact not only the cities in question but also the national economies which house them. This is so because metropolitan areas are known to house many of the modern sector activities which Third World economies must rely upon to accomplish their development objectives. Although various neoclassical thinkers may still be assuming that the population influx so evident in Third World urban areas is being prompted by opportunities for employment in modern sector activities, reality deviates regularly from that assumption. It deviates in the sense that the absorptive capabilities of the modern sector are somewhat limited at any point in time and in any case may not be able to accommodate the unskilled migrants who are entering urban labor pools. A second form of deviation from theoretical norms revolves around the fact that many migrants have few illusions concerning their marketability. In other words, objectives other than employment opportunities in the modern sector are prompting population movements. As a result, cities are growing in size much more rapidly than their capacity to absorb labor, and this circumstance is affecting them in ways that may interfere with their development, not to mention that of national economies.

When surplus labor relocates itself in urban settings, one of the more obvious results is the proliferation of slums. Certainly, growth in urban economies would occur more rapidly if surplus populations were left in rural areas. However, as seen from earlier discussions (Chapter 3), in most cases such a suggestion is unworkable. When migration into urban complexes continues, ongoing and increasing demands are made on the local economy for social overhead capital. Such demands may require a reordering of priorities on the part of local authorities. Such reorderings, with subsequent drains of public funds, can retard the provision of an infrastructure suitable for economic development. Of course, this in turn impedes the expansion of the modern sector and with that the ability of the economy to absorb labor. In some cases, drains on public funds do not stop at local coffers but instead invade national revenue pools, thus forcing adjustments in national priorities. Of course, this last scenario, where it occurs, is not the only way in which national development potential can be impacted by the urban influx. Since metropolitan areas house the strengths of national economies, the efficiency of those economies is impeded by anything that impairs the efficiency of the city.

In many metropolitan areas the mere positioning of housing for the poor can impede efficiency. In more advanced economies, slums have been an ongoing central city problem which seems resistant to the efforts of the planners. The fact that they have not disappeared in advanced nations is a reflection of the continuing existence of poverty rather than poor physical planning procedures. This being the case, Third World nations can hardly expect that slums can be eliminated any time soon. Since they exist in response to the housing needs of the poor, they are on the increase in metropolitan areas that are experiencing an influx of unskilled rural labor. Unlike slums in developed nations, housing for the urban poor in Third World jurisdictions often takes the form of squatter settlements. In many emerging nations squatter slums have become a phenomenon of the urban periphery. These settlements often develop around existing urban areas, sometimes beyond their political boundaries. Such agglomerations by their very existence can impose significant barriers on the growth of the urban economy.

In metropolitan areas impacted in this way, expansion of modern sector activities may intensify within the periphery, thus causing obvious difficulties with congestion. In other cases modern development may leapfrog over the slums, causing problems in transportation and communications, not to mention the provision of public services. Thus, the modern sectors of the city may face difficulties in becoming fully integrated. Assuming that such problems are solved, the slums will benefit from the new infrastructure which extends certain city services through them to reach expanding areas. By extending roads, water and sewerage, and other services through squatter settlements, the city gives such communities a greater degree of permanence. Whether this is good or bad must be assessed on a case-by-case basis.

At one time the current author was of the opinion that the major problem revolved around whether or not living conditions can be improved sufficiently so as to come in line with acceptable urban standards (McKee and Leahy, 1974). Unfortunately, the issue may be somewhat more complicated. Certainly slums which cannot be improved to where living conditions meet minimal urban standards can hardly be considered as necessary or even unavoidable participants in urban expansion. If slums or squatter settlements are constructed or positioned in a manner which interferes with the expansion of the urban infrastructure then they are not in step with the needs of urban expansion. Indeed, such communities will actually interfere with development.

"Because the slum occupies space and forces the expanding city to move beyond it, the urban infrastructure must expand geographically within an increasing cost framework" (McKee and Leahy, 1974). When a slum exhausts its ability to absorb more population there is a tendency for additional slums to form elsewhere. In some cases this may mean additional peripheral squatter settlements, but actually any open land may be at risk. If new settlements form a new urban periphery they may be followed in turn by new modern sector expansion beyond them. It may be thought that the innermost slums would gradually be assimilated into the city (McKee and Leahy, 1974), but such an assumption, where realized, may present long-run structural problems. If Third World metropolitan areas grow in this fashion, squatter settlements are actually determining both growth patterns and the eventual configuration of the urban complex.

Thus, it appears that the continuing influx of migrants from the countryside causes physical problems for recipient cities which go beyond the human problems that are in and of themselves considerable. Once the fledgling urbanites are in place they must be considered as part of the developmental mix. On the human side this may mean absorption into modern sector activities, but more realistically, it will mean the seeking of survival options in an urban informal sector characterized by squatter settlements. For the planners the new migrants and, for that matter, the cadres of veteran squatters must be regarded as a fait accompli. In a general sense the removal of squatters defies reality, and their continuing presence contributes to a set of problems actually caused by concentration.

"High on the list of problems associated with the urbanization of surplus labor is the fact that the increased population requires increased urban services" (McKee, 1982). Expenditures for various services will be increasing with no parallel increases in revenues. Certain basic services such as water and certain health-related items cannot be postponed. The provision of these and similar needs will result in an ad hoc rearrangement of government priorities which may impede general development efforts.

Despite their costs there may be ways in which slums, even those of the squatter variety, play positive roles in metropolitan complexes. New arrivals from the countryside, by congregating in urban settings, may enjoy services which would have been well beyond their reach in rural settings. Such things as inoculations and immunizations, not to mention health and safety education and even general basic education, can be provided more easily in concentrated urban circumstances. These and similar services may improve the chances of modern sector employment through increased productivity potential. Of course, this assumes that modern sector opportunities are becoming available.

The provision of the types of services alluded to above requires time, money, and expertise, and the utility of the squatter settlement will diminish if any of these factors are in short supply. The slum has long been recognized as a staging area for the urban poor (Frankenoff, 1967). Frankenoff saw slums as forming a vehicle for urban expansion which as such should be accepted and integrated into the urban community. He assumed slums to belong to growth processes in developing nations and to act as staging areas for the migrating poor. Recent support for such contentions may be drawn from the work of C. A. Tisdell. "Clearly the existence of the informal sector in the urban environment . . . acts as an attraction to would-be rural emigrants since, as a 'halfway house,' it provides prospects of some income while waiting for employment in the formal urban sector" (1990, 126).

Frankenoff saw the slum as a developing community as opposed to an existing one which is already developed (1967). He suggested that it was the interaction between the developing community and the existing one which causes economic expansion to proceed. It must be noted that there could be a downside to the type of interaction suggested by Frankenoff, a downside whereby the interaction between the developing community and an existing one stifles economic improvement. Frankenoff was optimistic, however, believing that by making the slum a part of the urban community it ceases to be a problem.

Almost by definition a staging area in the present context is a setting where new arrivals on the urban scene can position themselves during their assimilation into urban life. In advanced economies slums were thought to fulfill this function. Although slum residents had few of the amenities of urban life, their community was an optimistic place, since they viewed their problems or inconveniences as temporary. The solution on a personal level implied moving to more suitable surroundings (Stokes, 1962, 189 ff). In Third World settings lower levels of optimism may be indicated. Although some residents of squatter settlements do enter modern sector pursuits, over time many do not. Thus, the squatter settlements become more or less permanent habitats for those who inhabit them. Material improvements may occur in living conditions within specific settlements over time, but moving into the mainstream of the urban economy may mean upgrading the settlement rather than leaving it behind. In such cases noticeable human gains may not necessarily contribute to a stronger metropolitan economy, more capable of absorbing more workers, which may still be the most compelling scenario for those concerned with creating urban environments strongly supportive of continuing change and economic development.

The function of urban slums or squatter settlements and how to deal with them has often been misunderstood by those in planning or decision-making positions. "The use of military and/or heavy road machinery to eliminate squatter settlements in less developed countries" (McKee, 1982) has hardly been an effective planning tool. The lessons learned from the ineffectiveness of the "federal bulldozer" in urban America (Rothblatt, 1974) seem to apply in Third World settings. The general elimination of squatter settlements in the metropolitan complexes of emerging nations is hardly a viable policy option.

"There is no way of eliminating slums short of the elimination of poverty itself" (McKee, 1982). Since they are evidently an unavoidable and even necessary part of most metropolitan complexes, they should certainly be an integral part of the deliberations of planners and policymakers. Although it may be an enterprise laced with frustration, the planners should be concerned about the overproliferation of squatter settlements. Beyond that they should consider steps to ensure that the locating of the settlements does not interfere with the orderly and efficient development of the host city. It should be emphasized that the wholesale removal or shifting of existing settlements is hardly a viable option. This second planning directive can only be applied to the possible emergence of new settlements and perhaps to the expansion of those already in place. A third planning concern should be for provision of basic safety and human dignity for the inhabitants of the settlements. The objectives alluded to above have not been listed in a presumed order of importance. Sound planning would seem to require that they be given equal billing.

In keeping with the prescriptions enumerated above, it may not be advisable to provide for the gradual upgrading of settlements with an eye to graduating them from the genre. Such an objective, if successful, would probably ensure that as one area is being improved, others as bad or worse would be emerging. Any policy which may encourage a continuing fluctuation of conditions in the constituent parts of the metropolitan area will only result in additional uncertainties for the planners.

Major slum and squatter concentrations are an almost universal characteristic of Third World metropolitan areas. Their populations far exceed the absorptive capacity of modern sector labor markets. In most cases it is even difficult to obtain an accurate accounting of squatter populations. It seems certain however that squatter populations are growing as the exodus from rural areas continues.

In order to retard the growth of acreage given over to squatters, it seems important, where feasible, to encourage the residents of such communities to look beyond them as their material status improves. Douglas Butterworth and John K. Chance stated that squatters interviewed in Latin America indicated having settled in shantytowns "in order to send their children to school, to save on rent either by improving their present house or building another one, or to start a small business" (1981, 156). As these authors indicated, "None of these is a short-range goal and all indicate a hope or an ability to plan for the future" (156). Migrants entering squatter communities do not necessarily contemplate moving again.

In 1990 the current author accompanied an urban geographer to a squatter settlement located within walking distance of the central business district of Port of Spain, Trinidad. By returning to the location where the geographer had photographed the settlement years earlier and comparing his photographs to 1990 realities, substantial housing improvements were noted. Obviously, improvements lead to permanence and just as obviously the discouragement or prevention of improvements would appear to be counterproductive.

It seems safe to assume that improvements in housing and general living conditions will be accompanied by improvements in the financial or material status of residents. It was suggested earlier that the elimination of slums must await the elimination of poverty. What is true for slums in general is undoubtedly true for squatter settlements. Parallels between slums in advanced economies and squatter settlements in the Third World go further than that. Just as it can be said that not all slum residents in advanced economies are poor, the same material status sort holds true in squatter settlements. Squatter settlements contain highly heterogeneous populations (Butterworth and Chance, 1981, 156). "Residents may range from illiterate and chronically unemployed or underemployed to professionals such as lawyers and doctors" (Butterworth and Chance, 1981, 56, quoting Higgins, 1971, 19–38). Thus, it seems clear that many residents of squatter settlements may stay in such places well beyond the time when they were there by necessity. By doing so they are limiting the ability of existing settlements to absorb new migrants, thus contributing to the need for additional squatter accommodations.

Whether or not the circumstances described represent an over-proliferation of squatter settlements is an issue which should be examined by planners on a case-by-case basis. "Slums which are necessary have an upper limit bounded by the housing require-ments of the . . . poor . . . plus a suitable cushion to provide for new arrivals, laid off workers and others temporarily unemployed" (McKee, 1982). Unnecessary slums are unquestionably a drain on public funds and, beyond that, may very well interfere with the efficient expansion of urban complexes.

The way in which slums are located in metropolitan areas is an issue which has not received adequate attention. In Third World economies urban slums are often arranged haphazardly. As men-tioned earlier, they can take the form of squatter settlements around the urban periphery, as has been occurring in Latin Amer-ica. They can position themselves along rivers and in harbor areas, as have the floating slums of Asia. They can be housed within deteriorating urban neighborhoods. In Mexico City many squat-ters housed in warehouses and/or old industrial buildings were killed in a major earthquake. Squatters can also be housed in extended family compounds, as is rather common in parts of Africa. The above hardly exhausts the list of possible squatter configurations. Any combination of alternatives is possible. Squat-ter settlements are certainly the most unpredictable form of slum to deal with as they can vary in size from a few families to huge configurations embracing hundreds of thousands of residents. Another contributor to their unpredictability is the fact that they can appear almost anywhere.

The way in which peripheral slums can influence development patterns has already been discussed. A practical rule to apply to all slums would appear to be that they cannot be permitted to interfere with orderly metropolitan development. In this context the idea of supporting the improvement of slum property requires closer scrutiny. If slums are actually needed then it seems reasonable to suggest that their position within the urban complex should be planned as carefully as possible. In this way their negative impacts upon the metropolitan area can be minimized. Planners must also allow for the ability of squatters to reach potential work sites.

If these considerations are to be pursued it seems logical to plan for at least a minimum level of social overhead capital for the squatter settlements. Within certain limits it may also be acceptable to aid or encourage self-improvement programs on the part of squatters. It should be emphasized that any such programs should be in line with the goal of deciding where the slum should be and keeping it there. This, of course, seems to negate the idea of upgrading squatter settlements or slums to the point where they are eliminated. Generally, that practice appears to be ill-advised. Even in cases where there is a surplus of squatter accommodations, reducing them through upgrading may not be the way to go. It may be that a livable slum should be preserved as such rather than "improved," until it constitutes a rather marginal, middle-class community.

Surplus slums should be removed on a worst-first basis. Human dignity and safety are often problems in squatter communities. Unsafe slums must share top billing on any removal list with those that interfere with the efficient operation of the urban economy. Indeed, attention should be given to those two categories of settlements, even where there is no evidence that surplus slums exist. In extreme cases, steps to have them removed may be indicated. Safety threats may take many forms. Whether the threat stems from mud slides in Latin America, fires in Hong Kong, or floods in various Asian locations, it seems unreasonable to permit people to exist under such hazardous conditions. The lips of canyons or drop-offs in Central America, refuse dumps in the Middle East, or indeed the industrial buildings that collapsed in Mexico City are hardly acceptable human habitats. Examples such as have been enumerated here make the slum as a planning concept a significant idea and certainly not an oxymoron. The provision of conditions conducive to at least the minimum acceptable level of safety, not to mention human dignity, in necessary slums should be high in the pecking order of projects deserving outlays for social overhead capital.

The problem of burgeoning squatter settlements in Third World metropolitan areas must be solved within those urban complexes. As illustrated earlier in this volume (Chapter 2), there is little hope for the success of projects designed to take the pressure away from impacted areas by actually building new cities. Nor does it appear that inducements to direct surplus rural populations toward inter-mediate-sized cities will be successful. "In many nations such intermediate centers simply do not exist. Even where they do, the demonstration effect of the metropolis is difficult to diffuse" (McKee, 1982). Granted some rural residents may use smaller centers as an intermediate base, but eventually the pull of the larger cities entices them.

Even in areas where transportation, communications, and other services are improving, in rural areas such changes may hasten migration rather than providing an alternative to it. Improved access means improved knowledge of the city. As referred to earlier in this chapter, urban production facilities are actually putting smaller production units and handicrafts in smaller towns and rural areas out of business. Even where such small enterprises continue to exist, they are unlikely to impact the tide of migration in the long run. Commuting has even been suggested as a way of relieving population pressure (Brutzkus, 1975). Although there is some evidence of rural residents working in the city during the week and returning home on weekends, commuting as it exists in advanced nations hardly seems feasible.

With millions already in place in the squatter settlements of Third World metropolitan areas, and new arrivals augmenting their numbers day by day, planning may appear to be a hopeless or unrewarding process. Unfortunately, ignoring the issues associ-ated with the squatters, their needs, and their impact upon urban configurations may be the harbinger of even more insurmountable planning problems over the long run. Even the most conservative ideologues among development specialists should be able to real-ize the difficulties which they face. It seems clear that the transition of labor from rural to urban circumstances is hardly the orderly process which neoclassical modeling seems to suggest. Despite this it seems clear that market forces are driving the migrations which are swelling urban populations. It is the hope of survival and perhaps material improvement which is driving the population movements. As suggested earlier, stemming the flow appears to be unrealistic. Thus, development specialists and planners are left with the necessity of responding to the changes which are occurring if they hope to ensure that impacted urban areas can provide proper climates for economic expansion and improving human circumstances over time.

As difficult as the planning problems associated with burgeoning squatter populations appear to be, the situation may not be as hopeless as those who judge it by the standards of wealthier nations may believe. Nor is it the ringing refutation of neoclassical modeling that surface scrutiny may suggest. As has already been suggested, economic motives have large inputs with respect to the migration decisions which are driving the urban influx. "It may be . . . that migrants do not enter Third World metropolitan complexes armed with false hope of finding employment in the modern sector" (McKee, 1988, 29). Indeed "it may be that these new entrants to the urban labor market actually expect to improve their material welfare in spite of the very real shortcomings of employment in the informal sector" (29).

Thus, it is quite possible that neoclassical labor absorption models become more realistic if they are redirected to the informal sector. For the planners, the implications of this may be both good and bad. On the positive side, it seems clear that the residents of squatter communities, almost by the fact of their presence, have a certain grasp of economic self-interest. In theory at least they can be reached by appeals to that economic self-interest, which may make the human side of planning initiatives less difficult.

On the negative side, if informal sector activities are providing migrants with subsistence options and perhaps even opportunities for economic betterment over time, then continuing in-migration generates ever-increasing markets for what the informal sector has to offer. In such an optimistic climate in-migration will not just continue, it may very well accelerate. Of course, if continuing in-migration engenders competition on a level that makes survival more difficult, this may serve as a discouragement for it to continue (McKee, 1988, 30). With a modest contribution from hindsight, the current author now feels that the explanation involving an optimistic climate in the informal sector is the more realistic choice.

At this juncture the necessity of allowing for the positioning of squatter settlements or other living alternatives for the urban poor in metropolitan planning procedures is rather self-evident. As stated earlier, settlements can hardly be permitted to interfere with the efficient operation and growth of metropolitan areas. Nor should the continuation of dangerous living conditions be encouraged. Beyond the undesirable settlement patterns alluded to above there will undoubtedly be communities which realism demands should be considered as ongoing parts of the metropolitan mosaic. In addition, any comprehensive planning must allow for a continuing influx of people from the countryside.

Massive relocation projects involving squatter communities may be difficult if not impossible. Although some might believe public housing to be a reasonable solution, the costs in many instances would be prohibitive. Aside from the costs, difficulties with the administration of such facilities in advanced nations suggest caution. At best the winding down of unacceptable squatter settlements may be a long and difficult process.

Settlements which interfere with economic efficiency may be the easiest to deal with. In some cases the market may render some assistance. Perhaps the most obvious inefficiencies involve settlements on land which could be better used in ways which would expand modern sector activities which provide additional employment opportunities. In such cases land values in the settlements would be on the rise. Of course, this would be of little direct use to the squatters, since in most instances they will not have received title to the land which they are using. However, the market may render compensating them possible. If the land is publicly owned perhaps the squatters can be compensated monetarily for their housing and helped to move to areas selected by the planning authorities to house incoming migrants. If the planners have selected such areas wisely, additional enticements for squatters to move may include urban services such as the availability of piped water, some provision for the removal of human waste and garbage, and perhaps even access to small plots of land for growing of food crops.

The advantages to carefully chosen locations for poor communities include the possibility of making services such as those listed above available at reasonable public costs. If services are provided relatively free of charge, the areas become more attractive to potential residents, thus making the task of moving people from less desirable areas more manageable. In cases where settlements are on private land the market may well be able to compensate the squatters as part of the cost of transition.

If the inefficient location of communities involves encumbrances to integrating the metropolis rather than demands by the modern sector for the use of the land, problems may be more severe, at least initially. As mentioned earlier, for example, cases of leapfrog development in the modern sector cause problems with developing the necessary urban infrastructure. Urban services must be extended beyond the squatter communities in an increasing cost framework. This may mean electricity, water and sewage lines, and perhaps other services relating to education and perhaps safety. If existing roads must be widened or new ones built, this, of course, will add to the cost package. It should be mentioned that the use of highway construction as a slum clearance procedure has been tried in advanced nations with results that would hardly recommend it as something which should be considered. Roads should only be constructed or widened through squatter settlements if they are needed and no reasonable alternative routes are available. In cases where they are built, squatters displaced may be compensated liberally in exchange for moving to more suitable settlement locations discussed above.

Of course, services which are extended into newer urban areas beyond existing squatter settlements may be available to the settlements as well. This may make the settlements in question more attractive to their residents and thus more permanent. The only natural forces at work which might encourage their removal might be rising land values occasioned by better services or the general development of the urban area. In this latter case the policy scenario resembles that discussed earlier with respect to movements to more suitable locations compensated either from public funds or from the proceeds from private land sales. Failing to bring about such adjustments, those concerned with development should discourage new arrivals to the settlements in question while taking land abandoned by departing residents out of play. The movement of such communities by force seems ill-advised.

The same may not be true for settlements existing under dangerous conditions. International news services are replete with disasters involving squatters. It seems logical that settlements should be prevented from emerging in flood planes or on unstable hillsides, or areas prone to earthquake damage or ocean tidal surges. As obvious as such policy implications seem to be, it must be stated that people of considerable means are knowingly living in the path of such hazards in the wealthiest parts of the world. In Third World settings the types of locations in question are often of little economic significance and thus lend themselves to the development of squatter settlements. If they are to be removed the costs will fall on governments, since with few exceptions there is little chance of such land being valuable in the marketplace. Removal, as mentioned earlier, should be on a worst-first basis. There is no justification for permitting people to live in close proximity to airport runways or in the large water conduits to be found under highway interchanges. Such peculiar examples, however, only account for small portions of the problem. The removal of the problem of dangerous settlements is a long-range goal at best. Certainly potential sites which are dangerous should be policed or rendered inaccessible. The same is true for sites which are dismantled.

When land for new migrants has been apportioned and pecking orders have been established with respect to long-range plans for removing undesirable settlements, it remains to evaluate planning needs related to settlements which have been identified as ongoing parts of the metropolitan community. In these settlements certain public services should be provided. Some such services have been alluded to earlier, in connection with the establishment of new settlements. The services will establish a degree of permanence for the selected settlements. It should be emphasized that the permanence in question refers to positioning and needed services. As families or groups improve their material status they should be encouraged to move to better surroundings. In this way the settlements will be available over the long run to those who need them—new migrants and those who are still poor.

In positioning new settlements or retaining some which are already in existence, attention should be paid to the proximity of work opportunities. There is little point in housing the poor where no opportunities exist for them to enter the mainstream over time. In the short run it appears as though the poor in rather large numbers will have to work out their survival in the informal sector, something which they seem able to do. The current discussion will hardly solve the massive problems associated with the urban poor in Third World settings. Short of that, it should demonstrate the obvious need for careful planning. In the absence of such planning, the problems facing impacted metropolitan areas will only worsen. With that worsening impacted areas may lose the potential they hold to provide a climate for economic expansion.

5

Metropolitan Growth and the
Absorption of Urban Places

The issues raised in the previous chapter fall far short of exhausting the problems associated with burgeoning metropolitan areas in the Third World. Throughout the emerging nations urbanization and, more specifically, the growth of larger centers has been proceeding at rates far surpassing the ability of local economies to absorb new migrants. Aside from inadequate employment opportunities, in-migrants have triggered the emergence of various urban problems. Some such difficulties concern the welfare of the migrants themselves in the urban environment. They can run the range of personal needs from the basics of food and shelter to long-range considerations such as health and education. Other difficulties, which have been touched upon already in the preceding chapter, relate to the general needs of metropolitan complexes related to changing patterns of land use and service requirements. Of course, difficulties falling within the latter category pertain to the need for an ongoing ability to grow and change and remain efficient in the process.

"Irrespective of its cause ongoing population growth often places great stress on the infrastructures of urban complexes" (McKee, 1985). As might be expected, those concerned with development find themselves with ongoing difficulties with respect to the continuing viability of the local economy. Even if those concerned possess the financing to keep up with service requirements that are growing and changing, the physical problems associated with the supply function may well be substantial. Such difficulties are often further complicated by physical inflexibilities in urban forms.

As they grow in size cities are caught with narrow streets and difficult traffic patterns. Rising populations can lead to water and energy shortages. The ability to supply other essential services may be threatened as well, since government revenue sources frequently fail to keep pace. As was emphasized in the previous chapter, housing is a very complicated issue. When the absorptive capacity of existing slums is used up the new migrants will spill over into whatever unclaimed space presents itself. Despite the fact that local authorities are well aware of such difficulties, they may be ill equipped to stem the worsening conditions.

Certainly, economists and other social scientists are well aware of the magnitude of these and other problems associated with rising metropolitan populations. Economists in particular have been accused of having an urban bias and of ignoring even worse conditions which exist in rural areas. Perhaps it is the massive impacts which in-migration is having on Third World cities and not biases or preconceptions which are causing professional interest.

Sidestepping the debate about urban biases, the present chapter focuses on a set of problems which appear to be ignored by those concerned with patterns of urban expansion in the Third World. As metropolitan populations continue to grow it seems inevitable that the physical dimensions of those agglomerations expand as well. This expansion may even surpass what might be needed to accommodate the growing population. Even where commercial and industrial growth is slower than that of population, such activities will increase the physical size of urban complexes.

As the boundaries of urban complexes swell, more attention must be given to urban peripheries and to the physical directions and impacts of expansion. More particularly, attention must be given to what expansion at the periphery is doing to the cohesiveness and operating efficiency of the metropolitan complexes in question. One set of problems which must be considered is composed of the intricacies associated with the absorption of existing urban agglomerations as metropolitan peripheries move outward. Although models of Third World metropolitan expansion exist (e.g., Mohan, 1979) the issues alluded to appear to have been ignored. It appears as though a better understanding of them might assist economists and planners concerned with the growth and efficient operation of metropolitan complexes.

Earlier in this volume (Chapter 4) considerable attention was given to the impact of slums or squatter settlements on the urban periphery. The strictures which such settlements are placing upon the growth of the urban economy were discussed. The most basic issue revolves around the fact that squatter settlements on the periphery of metropolitan areas interfere with orderly expansion and establish increasing cost frameworks for expanding service infrastructures. Beyond that it was concluded that slums are actually dictating urban growth patterns. Unfortunately, there are other factors which may also interfere with growth patterns on the urban periphery. Prominent among those is the absorption of existing urban agglomerations with local functions, predating their forced marriage to the metropolis.

In wealthier nations the expansion of major metropolitan complexes is frequently characterized by the absorption of smaller centers which lose their spatial integrity in waves of urbanization. The absorption of these smaller urban areas creates an uneasy physical federation of urban places which often proves incapable of acting as a vehicle for the efficient provision of needed urban services, much less for ensuring that further expansion needs are met. Similar problems can emerge when existing urban areas are merged by transportation networks or the disappearance of open lands. Such mergers form multinucleated metropolitan areas with no apparent center of gravity. In the United States the Los Angeles metropolitan complex has been the prototype for the phenomenon, although a more identifiable city center has emerged in recent years.

The widespread interest in Third World metropolitan complexes has generated little concern on the part of investigators for the issues related to the absorption of smaller urban places. To some extent the same can be said for the phenomenon of the emergence of metropolitan complexes formed by the growing together of existing urban areas. It seems clear that the absorption of towns and cities, with a physical, social, and economic integrity independent of larger agglomerations, is adding new dimensions to the overall issue of uncontrolled urban expansion in Third World nations. Difficulties in human adjustment generated by such changes can easily be as severe in some cases as those facing migrants from rural areas. Certainly, these will have to be considered by the planners, together with the issues related to spatial absorption.

In some cases smaller urban centers are actually engulfed by the expanding metropolis. In other cases it may be that highway expansion makes land in the vicinity of small towns attractive for development. As land uses change, local residents become less able to meet their food needs from local sources. The commercial and service functions of impacted towns change dramatically. In some cases such functions may be eliminated in the new metropolitan environment. Thus, local labor markets suffer negative adjustments and those who were reliant upon them may quickly find their livelihoods threatened by the encroachment of the metropolis. The growing of food crops and small-scale animal husbandry may no longer be feasible. The same can be said for traditional produce marketing and other small-scale enterprises.

By their absorption into the metropolitan complex, small-town residents may find themselves suddenly without local services, not to mention income sources. Problems relating to transportation and perhaps even personal finances may make it difficult if not impossible for them to seek more sophisticated metropolitan substitutes. In a scenario not unlike what occurs in rural areas or towns at greater distances from major urban areas, younger or more ambitious residents may leave the towns in search of greater upward mobility in the metropolitan labor market. Such changes leave older and less capable residents to fend for themselves.

In spite of very real difficulties, smaller urban areas may be able to retain a certain physical integrity within the metropolitan mix. To an extent their abilities in this regard will depend upon the nature and positioning of new transportation facilities. If the transportation infrastructure that accompanies metropolitan expansion merely gives access to land around the small urban areas in question, their physical integrity may not be threatened. On the other hand, if the towns are actually on expanding highways the results may be more disruptive. For instance, in cases where existing roads are upgraded to modern highways, urban areas through which they pass may be irreparably changed. Such changes may include the actual destruction or removal of property which abuts the right of way. In some cases the changes may appear to be less severe but may include changing land-use patterns brought about by the fact that rising land values make it impossible for current owners to retain their holdings in their traditional functions. Under the best of circumstances it seems clear that highway systems, through a dramatic change in land values and in some cases even the physical makeup of the small communities through which they pass, can create a rather traumatic introduction to the metropolitan mosaic for the small communities in question.

The residents of impacted communities may find the integrity of their environment dramatically altered. In some cases they may even be displaced from their homes, but even where events fall short of that, the new traffic patterns and other negative externalities brought on by the advance of the metropolis may prove quite difficult to cope with. Jobs can be lost and long-standing commercial relationships destroyed, and town residents may find that they are no longer served or supported by the community where they are located. It seems clear that their future well-being will be directly related to their ability to become a part of the new metropolitan mix. In attempting to accomplish that they may be impeded by a lack of training and the immobilities associated with property ownership, not to mention various other personal considerations.

The probabilities are strong that the encroachment of the metropolis will destroy the economic and social integrity of smaller urban communities. Such areas may well survive in a physical sense but the ways of life of their residents may be irreparably altered. Some individuals may succeed in the new metropolitan climate, but others may falter and find themselves relegated to a metropolitan underclass (e.g., Santos, 1979). The latter group, having had their traditional methods of survival undermined, may be facing economic decline in a new and often hostile environment where living costs are rising and urban services may be inadequate.

In some ways this group may be less successful in dealing with their altered circumstances than are migrants from the countryside. The migrants, who may be fortified in some cases by unrealistic expectations, are better equipped in some ways for the life facing them in urban environments. They have come from rural circumstances which may have been far more devastating than those which they have adopted. Through moving into the squatter settlements they may be better positioned to survive in the informal economy of the metropolis than are those who have entered the metropolitan mix by default because their home communities have been absorbed.

It seems obvious that the absorption of peripheral towns can have chaotic impacts upon their residents, but such occurrences will also have significant effects upon the metropolitan areas themselves. It seems almost tautological to point to the population increases which cities are experiencing through absorbing smaller complexes. Another effect which may seem obvious is the swelling land areas encompassed by Third World metropolitan areas. This last consideration is an especially serious issue due to the fact that small urban enclaves, or some that are not so small, when added to expanding metropolitan complexes can cause major discontinuities in the metropolitan mosaic.

In a very real sense these smaller communities are like islands in a sea of urban land use and like islands they break up the continuity of the sea around them. In another similarity to islands they may cause a silting of activities around them in some cases. Like peripheral squatter communities (Chapter 4), they tend to interfere with the orderly expansion of urban space. As do the squatter settlements, they may cause problems for the continuity and efficient functioning of the metropolitan economy through difficulties in the efficient extension of transportation and service networks. When metropolitan expansion moves beyond them, the cohesiveness of the entire conurbation may be put at risk. From a metropolitan viewpoint the ongoing existence of small peripheral communities may be at odds with functional land-use patterns and, beyond that, may interfere with the functioning of the metropolitan economy.

Certainly, it would be impractical to consider the demolition or removal of small communities which are found to be in the path of metropolitan expansion. Short of that, negative impacts from their merger with the metropolis can be reduced by careful, advanced planning. Unfortunately, in most cases little attention is being paid to this issue in Third World economies. In fairness it must be said that the absorption of communities peripheral to major metropolitan complexes in wealthier nations has hardly been receiving extensive attention among planners. Such mergers are simply allowed to occur. The difficulties which emerge seem to be treated on an ad hoc basis as they assume serious proportions.

The only transferable knowledge to be gleaned from events in wealthier nations appears to be the aging dictum concerning an ounce of prevention. In Third World settings, by paying careful attention to the positioning of transportation and service facilities, it might be possible to direct metropolitan expansion away from such communities. In some cases small towns can be bypassed. The practicality of such alternatives depends to a large extent upon the size and positioning of the communities in question. In cases where physical mergers are inevitable, major priority must be given to the efficient provision of services in the metropolitan region as well as to the extension of the metropolitan infrastructure, according to the dictates of efficiency and cohesiveness.

On a field trip to San Juan, Puerto Rico, the author was able to observe certain older communities (barrios)[1] on the periphery of the metropolitan area. Because the small urban communities in question were located on hilly ground they had been able to maintain their local identity as the metropolis expanded around them. Their access to the metropolis was through freeway networks passing nearby. There was no obvious evidence that their proximity to the city was impacting them negatively. From the viewpoint of orderly or efficient metropolitan growth the observed enclaves were no problem, since the land which they occupied was hardly suitable for redevelopment. In other words, to a large extent, whatever difficulties the positioning of the barrios might have caused for metropolitan planners would have occurred in their absence due to the nature of the landscape.

Unfortunately, the happy coincidence of circumstances outlined above is hardly the norm. The communities in question were positioned near the southern extremity of the Puerto Rican metropolis. Toward the east and west developmental disruptions were evident in rather large urban areas, the existence of which obviously predated the emergence of the present-day metropolis.

Such disruptions may be much more prevalent than orderly metropolitan assimilation.

Although San Juan has been absorbing existing communities on its periphery and even now appears to be reaching out to Chaguas to the south, its overall development seems to have been cast in the mold of a smaller Los Angeles, whereby the metropolis has emerged from the growing together of a number of existing communities. Although water barriers have caused some integration problems for the metropolis, the planners have done rather well in the positioning of highways and in assigning the direction of street traffic to meet the demands of rush hours. The old colonial city with its narrow streets has undergone a graceful alteration of functions, whereby it now serves as a monument to earlier times, while the main commercial functions of the metropolis have moved elsewhere. In its capacity as a living museum the old colonial city still provides housing for a fairly dense urban population while serving as a locus for tourist-oriented shops and restaurants. Positioned as it is on a promontory near the harbor mouth, and separated from portions of the metropolis by the harbor, it hardly serves as an actual central city or the fulcrum around which the metropolis is continuing its development.

Because of the specifics of the relationship which Puerto Rico holds with the United States, the island economy hardly conforms in any general way to Third World economies of similar size. Nonetheless, the makeup of the San Juan metropolitan area does provide useful insights on how an integrated metropolis can emerge from the coming together of smaller agglomerations. As has been the case in Third World economies, Puerto Rican urban areas have been experiencing an influx of population. In San Juan poorer elements of the population have access to public housing; thus, squatter settlements are a very minor contributor to the physical makeup of the urban complex.

Emergent Third World metropolitan areas formed by the coming together of existing urban communities may not be as fortunate. If such areas become the destination of migrating surplus labor the integration of the emerging metropolitan centers may be impaired. Incoming migrants will take the line of least resistance in selecting sites to settle, with the one proviso that the chosen site offers reasonable survival options. Thus, they will locate near modern sector job opportunities where such exist. In this respect, access to the leading center in the emerging complex and/or secondary centers may prove attractive if jobs in the service sector seem to be attainable. In multinucleated metropolitan areas, service opportunities may be more accessible than is the case in centers of comparable size which have a more conventional central business district. This being the case, potential absorption into entry-level modern sector jobs may be a stronger population magnet in multinucleated metropolitan areas. Beyond such considerations, migration decisions based upon survival options in the informal sector may still be important.

The multinucleated metropolis in the process of development may be an especially attractive destination for migrants. Open land, where it still exists between existing urban nuclei, provides good access for squatters. Not only do they have housing locations available but they have flexibility in terms of where in the general configuration of the building metropolis they may wish to locate. Beyond this, open land provides the opportunity for rather large squatter communities to emerge, enhancing opportunities in the informal sector. Thus, multinucleated metropolitan areas may well become impacted by in-migrants because of perceived opportunities in both service pursuits and informal sector activities. Where there is substantial manufacturing activity in place this may only broaden the attractiveness of the area for migrants.

In advanced nations major metropolitan areas suffer from various planning problems occasioned by multiple jurisdictions. In Third World settings appropriate planning bodies, with or without any real controlling power, are often nonexistent. In the absence of such professional intervention, the types of metropolitan expansion discussed above seem destined to generate major physical difficulties for emerging metropolitan areas. Clearly, economic integration and the ongoing provision of urban services can become major problems once the multinucleated conurbation comes together, as evidenced by the disappearance of open land between its constituent parts. Planning intervention with the overall efficiency of the emerging metropolis in mind is indicated as early as feasible. Because of potential difficulties in getting a working planning authority together that is representative of the constituent nuclei, it may be advisable for a higher authority to assume the needed planning role. Perhaps a federal agency, if given the charge, might be better able to make decisions in the interest of the metropolitan configuration as a whole.

High on the list of needed planning goals is an infrastructure which integrates the emerging complex with allowances for its ongoing expansion. Beyond that would be the provision of urban services on a uniform basis throughout the complex. Such services should include safe water, electricity, and a provision for the handling of sewage and other waste materials. Provision must also be made for services related to production facilities as well as decisions concerning where additional facilities should be placed and serviced.

As planning procedures are developed to provide for the physical concerns listed above, attention must also be given to incoming migrants. As referred to in the preceding chapter, this involves, among other things, both the positioning and servicing of squatter settlements. Ruling out public housing on practical grounds, once again the planners are faced with the necessity of controlling the location of new arrivals. In the case of multinucleated metropolitan areas they may have more flexibility in that regard. By acting quickly they can encourage the settlements to form in areas which are still open and safe. By acting quickly they can insure that the new arrivals are adequately positioned with respect to access to work and also with respect to the supply of basic service needs. Quick action ensures as well that squatters will not impede the construction of highway linkages and other needed infrastructure projects.

At times it is possible for Third World nations to benefit from the experience of wealthier nations. In the case of what has been outlined above, such transfers of knowledge may not be feasible. As mentioned earlier, much which comes under the heading of urban and metropolitan planning in advanced nations is cast in the mold of crisis response. Developed on an ad hoc basis, such responses are often ill considered. In the United States examples of such ill-conceived actions abound in the case of urban renewal and slum clearance.

It hardly seems appropriate for Third World metropolitan areas to assume the crisis-response method of planning. No doubt there will be more than an adequate supply of opportunities for such responses, but planning must be rescued from this modus operandi. Many crises can be avoided by careful planning. This should certainly be the case in many circumstances referred to in this chapter. If multinucleated metropolitan areas are permitted to emerge without assistance, and if metropolitan areas are permitted to move outward from their boundaries like tsunami, then certainly plans of action for crisis response will be needed.

Unfortunately, the diffusing of crisis conditions as they occur will hardly provide for an orderly and efficient local economy. Much could be accomplished if the diseconomies inherent in small-town absorption could be reduced by advanced planning. Much could be accomplished with respect to securing a well-integrated, multinucleated metropolis through advanced planning. Where planning is absent or limited, areas which come together to form large agglomerations may be implicitly subjecting themselves to the problems which may be latent in a fledgling Los Angeles, without gaining any potential advantages in return.

NOTE

1. In some Latin American countries barrios are squatter settlements. In Puerto Rican parlance the term can refer to neighborhoods or perhaps small communities.

6

Environmental Issues in an Urban Context

U rban expansion is emerging as a recognized contributor to environmental problems on a worldwide basis. "The problems of pollution and environmental damage both within and as wrought by urban areas have recently become matters of public concern as a part of the generally increased awareness of the public concerning environmental issues" (Walker, 1981, 225). Walker suggested that the quality of the natural environment should concern an urban society for at least two reasons. To begin with, natural environments are essential to the functioning of cities. Second, "the reduction in the ability of the natural environment to cope with the effects of urbanization increases costs for urban dwellers" (226). Walker was talking in terms of conditions in wealthier nations. In the Third World it appears as though a reduction in the coping ability of the natural environment with respect to urbanization may actually impair both growth and development.

Marcia D. Lowe is even more general in voicing her concern for the way in which cities impact natural environments. "The way cities physically evolve—and the way their development is planned—has profound impacts on human and planetary well-being" (1992, 119). She goes on to state that the further growth of cities "can either recognize the limits of the natural environment, or it can destroy the resources on which current and future societies depend" (119–120). Cities are clearly necessary for any functioning economy, but it seems clear that cities with mismanaged environments can create problems, both economic and physical, which may have repercussions well beyond their boundaries.

According to Tisdell (1990, 134), "Industrialization and urbanization of the Third World can be expected to create environmental problems for the whole world." He was speaking of impacts of circumstances where industrialization and urbanization were specifically associated with increased energy use, but surely his observation deserves a more general application. With respect to increased energy use Tisdell suggests that substantial increases in the consumption of fossil fuels (presumably in Third World urban areas) "will increase the serious likelihood of climatic change . . . increase urban air pollution, raise the prevalence of acid rains and acidification, and add to environmental problems and risks" (134). As Tisdell suggests, "The developed world cannot ignore the environmental impact of the urbanization and industrialization of the Third World, given the environmental global interdependence of the modern world" (134). Assuming the accuracy of his position, it would appear that Third World nations ignore environmental considerations associated with urbanization, at their own peril.

In wealthier nations large metropolitan areas are replete with major environmental difficulties. The most visible among those may be emissions from automobiles and industrial processes. Such airborne pollutants have attracted attention well beyond their urban origins, since they are hardly respecters of political boundaries. Other forms of industrial pollution, which foul river systems and water tables and land areas which have become receptors of abandoned or jettisoned wastes and industrial cast-offs, have also attracted public attention. Problems have emerged with respect to the sensible disposal of industrial waste and waste in general. In the United States, for example, the landfills which service major metropolitan areas are approaching their capacities, prompting the interstate shipment of municipal waste. Beyond waste there is the problem of sewage which, in the case of the United States, has on occasion threatened both Atlantic and Pacific coastal areas, indicating that the treatment of such materials has been less than adequate.

Beyond the rather obvious difficulties cited above are some that may seem less immediately or obviously worrisome. Walker referred to various ways in which urbanization may be expected to impact the atmospheric environment: "First, by covering surfaces with brick, concrete and metal, so that heat and atmospheric aerodynamics are affected" (1981, 225). He also mentioned the emission of both solid and gaseous pollutants and the generation of large amounts of heat. This last concern is especially serious since "Cities tend to generate 'heat islands'—which tend to lock within them circulatory air, thus reducing the pollution-dispersing power of the atmosphere" (225–226).

In the Third World, large, rapidly expanding urban complexes are emerging "whose sheer size and instability create problems on an entirely different scale" (Lowe, 1992, 121). According to Lowe, as early as 1980 seven of the world's ten largest cities were in the Third World (121). In the Third World some of the problems alluded to earlier in this chapter may be even more difficult to deal with, given the shortage of funds and, in some cases, apathy on the part of those in control. Indeed, some of the environmental difficulties generated by certain types of production may be viewed as a necessary evil by those concerned with expanding the modern sectors of Third World economies.

The level of environmental difficulties facing Third World metropolitan areas would appear in part to be an increasing function of the size of the urban complexes in question. Of course, other factors may be influential as well. For example, climate and topography may have parts to play to the extent that they impact the ability of natural forces to reduce environmental difficulties. The industrial mix may also be an important factor in some cases. Nonetheless, these and other factors not directly related to city size render environmental management more difficult when they converge in major Third World metropolitan areas.

As Tisdell has suggested, "Urbanization and industrialization generally lead to the concentration of wastes in a locality" (1990, 133). He was speaking of wastes from production processes as well as those generated by humans. He sees such concentrations as untracking natural ecological processes, thus necessitating the introduction of artificial means (e.g., sewage treatment) and public regulation. Failure to intervene, he suggests, may impact health and may even adversely affect production through "environmental spillovers or externalities" (153). Faced with such unpleasant possibilities, Tisdell states that "Environmental factors need to be taken into account in the planning of urban developments and in determining optimum locations, size, and rates of growth of urban areas" (133). Although Tisdell's prescription seems deserving of attention, there is little evidence that his concerns have been reflected in any general way in policies implemented by those concerned with the planning of Third World metropolitan areas.

Martin T. Katzman suggested that rapid environmental change generates public managerial problems (1977, 174). In a rural setting he saw "the pressures created by rapid population growth on public managers" to be relatively minor (174–175). The reason given is that in rural environments "little is invested in large-scale infrastructure and congestion and pollution are less salient" (174). Presumably, rural residents might be better able to cope as individuals with the type of environmental diseconomies (e.g., congestion and pollution) which Katzman was considering.

According to Katzman, population expansion in urban settings is much more prone to generate difficulties for public managers. He saw rapid population growth in urban settings as creating "automatic pressures on public managers as the water supply becomes contaminated, garbage piles up on the streets, conflagrations devastate neighborhoods, and traffic comes to a standstill" (175). He saw such pressures as proportional to the rate of growth as opposed to the mere size of the population. In taking that position he was, of course, giving implicit recognition to the inflexibilities of infrastructure components faced with population growth.

In the components of urban infrastructures concerned with maintaining and enhancing the environment, such rigidities may interfere with growth potential. Population pressure in such circumstances may render the climate hostile to modern sector activities and labor absorption (see McKee, 1991a). Katzman saw the difficulties which he posited as "almost as acute in small cities as in large ones and in countries with low shares of urban population as in those with high shares" (175). If Katzman was correct, urban environmental difficulties can hardly be ignored by planners who see the city as the setting for expanding modern sector activities and thus both growth and development.

Third World metropolitan areas are experiencing environmental difficulties in two specific areas which surpass the environmental difficulties facing large cities the world over. To ensure that their urban complexes provide healthy settings for economic expansion, planners in Third World nations must solve these difficulties as well as the general difficulties associated with urban environments. A unique set of problems with environmental overtones revolves around the continuing influx of population which most major Third World urban agglomerations are facing. The second set of difficulties facing the planners are those generated by industrial facilities. As mentioned earlier (Chapter 3), much of the population influx finds housing in squatter settlements which position themselves in unpredictable ways within metropolitan complexes. Problems which such developments cause for the city as a whole with respect to economic efficiency and growth potential have been alluded to earlier. It remains here to deal with the specifics of the environmental issues that such settlements raise.

Katzman was correct in suggesting that "the effective demand for most municipal services is generally exerted in the neighborhoods where people live, not in the city as a whole" (1977, 176). In-migrants who position themselves in squatter settlements do not automatically create an overload situation with respect to the provision of public services in general in the metropolitan complex. As Katzman has suggested, "Whether or not migrant areas are served is an explicit political decision" (176). In many Third World settings squatters may enjoy few of the urban services which may be taken for granted in more affluent areas. In terms of environmental matters, service options and priorities deserve a closer scrutiny. Abstracting from arguments couched in humanitarian terms for the moment, it should be noted that negative externalities of an environmental nature are hardly respecters of political or economic boundaries.

The sheer magnitude of squatter components in Third World metropolitan complexes suggests that environmental difficulties spawned in the settlements can hardly be ignored. Lowe has estimated that "illegal communities hold 30–60 percent of the population of many Third World cities" (1992, 122). She suggests that "planners in the Third World's giant cities face colossal environmental problems," which include a gamut of those with industrial origins "to the actual sinking of cities such as Bangkok, Jakarta, and Shanghai due to overdrawing of groundwater" (122). If Lowe is correct, the potential for environmental difficulties originating in squatter settlements is increasing in Third World metropolitan areas, since "an estimated 70–95 percent of new housing in most Third World cities is unauthorized" (170). Clearly, governments must consider the potential environmental implications of this in their planning deliberations.

Despite the fact that planners can, at least in theory, withhold any or all municipal services from squatter settlements, in practice in the case of some services and some settlements it may make little sense to do so. If, as suggested earlier (Chapter 3), planners should try to control the positioning of settlements in keeping with the growth and development of an economically viable metropolitan complex, the provision of certain services may be an effective tool. Certainly the provision of piped water and even access to electricity may serve to encourage population expansion in the areas selected by the planners.

Unfortunately, excluding certain areas from service grids may not produce population declines. A lack of public services in many urban environments is a condition which millions of squatters may expect and accept. Citing information concerning Sao Paulo, Katzman pointed out that a complete range of services was available only in the central, wealthier areas (1977, 176). He found that 84 percent of the households in that city were served by water and refuse collection but only 60 percent by sewerage services. He suggested that the "availability of these services to lower income peripheral areas is less in less-advanced cities" (176).

Significant questions raised by Katzman which are still relevant today were "to what extent urban public services provided to migrants are a gratuitous drain on resources and to what extent they increase present and future levels of welfare" (177). Such questions seem especially pertinent when applied to services that impact urban environments. The implication seems to be that services which may be appreciated by their recipients and commendable on humanitarian terms may be withheld if they contribute little to the developmental needs of the urban complex. An example of the type of service referred to above may be electricity. Such a service is clearly beneficial to those who can access it. However, where it is not provided residents will find ways to cope with its absence.

On the other hand, there may be services the withholding of which may seriously impact urban complexes. This category of services would clearly include provisions for the disposal of sewerage and other forms of waste. Residents of squatter settlements will hardly want to be impacted by sewerage and garbage. In the crowded confines of squatter settlements options are limited with regard to sewerage disposal. Dealt with improperly, such discharges, aside from creating an unpleasant living environment, can contaminate water supplies, encourage insect populations, and perhaps foster disease. Any or all of these unpleasant externalities can have impacts upon urban complexes which are hardly confined to the settlements that generate them. Of course, this is not to suggest that such negative externalities would be acceptable if confined to the settlements in question but rather to endorse the logic that, since they are not confined to such areas, they can be considered to be legitimate concerns for metropolitan-wide planning authorities.

In the absence of sewerage removal services the residents of the settlements will be forced to rely upon their own devices. Generally, such solutions will be geared to the topography or physical configuration of the land embraced by or accessible to the settlement. Settlements on hillside slopes may rely upon drainage ditches or latrines designed to take advantage of gradients. However efficient such disposal systems may be, they will result in buildups of sewerage at the bottom of gradients. Water courses, where available, may prove to be more successful disposal systems, but they themselves will become contaminated with unpredictable results for the urban complex. Privies or common disposal sites may hold an advantage if they contain the problem and limit the area impacted, but such solutions may result in problems with groundwater. Clearly, the safe and efficient disposal of human wastes within the confines of squatter settlements is a serious issue. The potential for difficulties may increase exponentially with the size of the settlements concerned.

It would appear that the removal of sewerage from squatter settlements is an example of a public service that the planners would be well advised to provide. Whether that means the provision of public privies which access waste drains or the removal of waste by tanker trucks, failure to address the issue may have repercussions throughout the urban areas. In cases where settlements empty their sewerage into water courses directly, the communities in question may have to be placed upon lists of dangerous settlements which are candidates for removal (Chapter 3). This is certainly true of the floating slums to be found in the rivers and harbors of Asia. Of course, it goes without saying that the removal of sewerage from squatter settlements will have the largest positive impact upon the urban complex only if it is subsequently treated prior to being released. Failure to treat sewerage can have dire environmental consequences, especially in tropical settings.

A seemingly related issue in squatter settlements pertains to the treatment of garbage and cast-off materials. Squatters may well find some advantage in locating at or near metropolitan garbage dumps. Many of the urban poor in Third World settings may augment their meager means through salvaging cast-off materials. In such settings many abandoned materials may command a price and/or provide utility to those recovering them. Indeed, in some cases the recovery of materials by the poor reduces the ongoing pressure on metropolitan dump sites.

Despite real economic gains to be had by those willing to pick over metropolitan garbage, negative externalities may be present as well. Dump sites may be inhabited by vermin which may endanger those relying upon such sites for their salvage activities. Such dangers are especially significant where children are concerned. Even in the absence of vermin there may be physical damage associated with dump sites. Cuts and abrasions incurred can lead to serious illness and even death. Dangers may exist in food and animal matter to be found at dump sites. Aside from being a source of contamination themselves, such materials attract insects which may become secondary suppliers of infection and disease. Clearly, entire squatter populations are hardly at risk due to their interest in dump sites. Nonetheless, it may be in the interests of metropolitan authorities to incinerate garbage or at least to provide for safe and inaccessible disposal sites. Beyond that, it may be that squatter settlements should not be encouraged in close proximity to dump sites.

Because of the extent of squatter settlements in Third World metropolitan areas, the garbage which they generate should be of major concern. Even though many such settlements feature homes built of scavenged materials and their residents seem judicious in salvaging or preserving useful items, such densely settled areas generate considerable cast-off material. If garbage is left to decay in the settlements it may attract vermin and may also become a source of disease or infection. If the residents are left to their own devices garbage may be disposed of in a haphazard fashion. It may come to block storm drains and culverts and, like human waste, may find its way into waterways and harbors. If residents tend to dispose of it by burning, fire hazards are present, not to mention dangers from air pollution. As is the case with human waste it would seem advisable that public authorities make provision for the safe disposal of garbage. User charges may not be feasible in the case of the inhabitants of squatter settlements. Nonetheless, disposal by the metropolitan authorities deserves priority, since failure in that regard may generate extensive negative externalities which might well be capable of untracking efficient development.

It seems clear that certain services must be provided to the inhabitants of squatter settlements in the interests of overall economic efficiency. Beyond those discussed above, the provision of safe water should also be considered. Water, under crowded conditions, is easily contaminated and can become a source of various diseases which can easily spread through metropolitan populations. Thus, safe water is certainly an important underpinning for a functional urban environment. It can hardly be pumped into every modest dwelling in evidence in Third World settings, but by providing piped water, accessible by pumps in strategic locations in urban squatter settlements, the quality of life and the environment that is prevalent can be improved substantially, to the benefit of the entire metropolitan complex.

It is clearly impractical to suggest that squatter settlements can be turned into environmental garden spots. Short of that, however, they can be made safer and somewhat more pleasant if the issues above are addressed. Refusal to deal with such problems will in many cases impede growth and development in metropolitan complexes, and to the extent that such complexes house the leading sectors of the national economy, it may retard advances at that level as well. All environmental issues involving squatter settlements must be weighed and prioritized in keeping with the needs and objectives of general development. Certain settlements adjudged to be dangerous on environmental grounds must be added to the list of those given priority for removal (Chapter 4).

The second set of problems impacting urban environments in the Third World stems from industrial sources. Often the manufacturing facilities that are fouling the environment are components of multinational firms. In some cases the decision by such firms to locate in Third World settings was prompted in part by permissive attitudes on the part of public authorities in host jurisdictions toward activities and processes which threaten the environment. As advanced economies become less sympathetic toward such production facilities, it seems less than surprising that they relocate in more accommodating settings.

Industrial pollution is reaching levels in Third World urban areas where public authorities are being forced to take a hand. A recent pollution emergency in Mexico City, which boasts some 30,000 factories, forced some of the worst polluters to reduce production by 30 percent (*Plain Dealer*, March 29, 1992, 46). On the level of public policy it would seem advisable for potential host governments to establish some understandings with those wishing to locate industrial facilities. Among the components of such needed understandings, environmental concerns are becoming increasingly significant.

Since political constituencies in wealthier nations are becoming increasingly vocal concerning industrial polluters, it is hardly surprising that some corporate decision makers are electing to relocate dirtier production processes in Third World jurisdictions. In accepting such enterprises host nations are obviously making a trade-off between a certain amount of environmental degradation and the growth which such production units may generate. Few economists would ever advise a Third World economy to opt for a zero level of industrial pollution. Economic historians are well aware of the environmental difficulties that the now-developed world faced during the industrial revolution. In some locations, industrial cities for instance, those difficulties were acute, but history has not shown them to have been irreversible. Thus, many economists would endorse the hosting of industrial polluters by Third World jurisdictions. However, those engaged in development planning in such jurisdictions should examine the potential advantages and disadvantages of every proposal put before them, in advance of accepting polluting facilities.

In some circles an international welfare calculus is being applied in enthusiastic support of the Third World as host to operations which foul local environments. In a recent editorial, *The Economist* (February 15, 1992, 18–19), in a not entirely enthusiastic vein, summarized the content of an internal memo from Lawrence Summers, chief economist of the World Bank. It highlighted three main points attributed to Summers: "First, the costs of pollution depend on earnings forgone through death or injury; these costs are lowest in the poorest countries" (18). Beyond that, costs rise disproportionately with pollution, such that moving pollution from dirtier to cleaner settings reduces costs. Finally, the appreciation of a clean environment rises with income such that, ceteris paribus, "costs fall if pollution moves from rich places to poor ones" (18).

Hopefully, as *The Economist* reported, the World Bank accurately interpreted Summers as "merely trying to provoke debate" (18). Certain elements of Summers' position require little attention here. However, from the point of view of potential host jurisdictions, the argument that pollution costs of various types are less for whatever reasons than they would have been in wealthier nations may not constitute a good reason for Third World jurisdictions to accept specific polluting activities. As *The Economist* suggests, "All three arguments [of Summers] share a distinctively economic premise: environmental policy involves trade-offs, and should seek a balance between costs and benefits." Such a balance will be different in every Third World setting and for each proposed activity. Planners concerned with this balance in specific settings must construct their equations in keeping with the needs of their domestic economy rather than the fact that pollution costs to them are less than would be the case for wealthier nations hosting such activities.

The Economist correctly recognizes that pollution controls are costly and benefits may be small in certain Third World settings (18). In such locations pollution-creating activities may be justified, depending upon their positive impacts and their relative costs. In some cases expanded employment opportunities and thus growth may have to be weighed against short-run negative externalities and environmental damage which may be both costly and permanent. Such a calculus may well demonstrate the hosting of certain polluters to be justifiable.

Planners in Third World jurisdictions who elect to accept dirty production facilities are presumably doing so on rather pragmatic grounds. The very pragmatism which encourages or justifies their decisions seems to fall short of supporting the acceptance of polluters because the operations of such polluters are less costly in poorer nations. Reducing pollution costs in wealthier nations should hardly concern the planners unless they can turn that result to their advantage in terms of compensation or some other visible gains for their nations. Jurisdictions where as little as 20 percent of the population may be plugged into the market economy can hardly be expected to join voluntarily in some sort of welfare synthesis which anoints them as the guarantors of the environmental welfare of the developed world.

Within Third World nations electing to encourage or accept pollution-ridden production processes, decisions must still be made with respect to the location of such activities. Allowing them to locate in major metropolitan areas may not be cost effective. Less-congested locations may be more advantageous for reasons similar in some cases to those advanced by Summers. Certainly, the polluters should have less of an impact on human populations if they are located away from metropolitan areas. The feasibility of nonmetropolitan locations is, of course, constrained by the infrastructure.

Certainly, market forces on their own should tend to concentrate economic activities in general in urban settings. This is no doubt what has been occurring in Mexico City, which has been operating under crisis conditions. Such extreme circumstances seem to suggest a lack of sound planning. Mexico City is hardly alone in experiencing such conditions. The present author was recently in a Third World urban area where airborne chemical pollutants sickened school children to an extent that the schools had to be closed. Such circumstances should perhaps not be justified by the supposition that the children in question suffered losses less severe and/or extensive than their counterparts in advanced nations might have experienced under similar circumstance.

There appear to be no easy solutions to environmental difficulties in Third World metropolitan areas. The elimination of such difficulties is hardly possible, nor would it be recommended as a goal by most economists. Nonetheless, environmental concerns deserve a place in the planning agenda. Certainly, environmental difficulties which impede economic growth and development must be addressed. It has been suggested that "Many Third World nations may consider environmental restraint as an expensive luxury, well beyond their financial means" (McKee, 1991b, 188). If this posture is adopted in congested urban areas, growth and development may be retarded and permanent environmental damage may be incurred.

Part III

Selected Structural Issues

7

Production for Export and Urban Flexibility

Many jurisdictions which are categorized as constituent parts of the Third World today are former colonies or territories controlled by wealthier and more powerful nations. The demise of traditional imperial systems has left many of those jurisdictions independent but impoverished. A partial explanation for their predicament rests with the fact that the economies which these now independent nations inherited were hardly designed for the purpose of generating viable independent nations. In a very real sense they functioned as overseas appendages to well-established economies. In many cases they existed as sources of supply for raw materials, foodstuffs, and other primary commodities needed by the developed world.

Although many Third World nations have continued to export primary commodities, their role in the international economy is changing. As independent nations they now have responsibilities associated with growth and development, or, more specifically, they must find the means to strengthen their economies in ways which will improve the living standards of their people. In pursuing their goals it seems inevitable that they must continue to deal in the international economy. It is also inevitable that such dealings will impact their economies and their prospects for development. It may also be that foreign linkages, past and present, will impact the urban sectors of Third World economies. If that is the case, the interplay between external linkages and urban economies deserves careful consideration if the planners are to be successful in facilitating ongoing development.

Although development planners in Third World economies may have thought that political independence would signal economic independence as well, few would deny the necessity for an international involvement on the part of the jurisdictions they represent. Certainly, the impact of the rest of the world on the welfare of less-developed areas is hardly a new area of concern for economists. Insights on the subject can be traced as far back as the writings of the Mercantilists. In recent years economists have displayed a great deal of interest, the tangible results of which can be seen in a flood of works on such matters as the balance of trade, import substitution, foreign aid, and, of course, the impacts of multinational corporations.

In this chapter the focus will be on the impacts which external forces or linkages are having upon the nature of infrastructures in Third World settings and, more specifically, the impacts which they are having on urban complexes and thus on overall development potential. In search of such insights three separate, yet perhaps related, phenomena will be considered. First of all, the role played by staple commodities will be considered. Following that the impact which dualism may have on developmental infrastructures will be discussed. Finally, the special impacts from foreign-owned production facilities will be explored.

As has been suggested above, the need for various staple commodities was often a major causal element in generating contact between the more advanced nations and areas of the world which were less fortunate. As far back as the time of the Mercantilists precious metals were procured in less-developed areas and brought to Europe to enhance the coffers of royalty. Spices and gemstones were procured from Asia and Africa. North America became a source of furs and fish, not to mention plantation crops. During the Napoleonic era that continent also supplied masts for the British navy. Most procurement efforts relating to primary commodities were basic extractive procedures, which depleted the natural resources of various areas. The intent of the procuring powers had little to do with the development of staple-producing locations.

Despite the obvious lack of interest on the part of the former colonial powers in any form of broad-based development in staple-producing territories, some development did occur in certain jurisdictions where staples were being produced. This type of development was geared specifically to procuring the commodities sought and getting them back to the controlling nations. The inheritance from such policies is certainly still in evidence in vast areas of North America. Whether Third World nations tracing their economic roots to staple exports can use those roots as the foundation for sustained economic advances is hardly self-evident.

In certain areas of the world there is little doubt that the pursuit of staples did influence the pattern of development. In fact, in this century economic historians have crafted an explanation for expansion based upon staple exports. The originator of this line of discussion was Harold Innis, a Canadian economist, who studied the part played by staple exports in the development of his own country (Innis, 1954 and 1956). In a similar vein, Douglass North has depicted economic expansion in the United States as a capitalistic venture centered largely upon exploitation (North, 1970). North saw the settlement of the United States to be the result of a search for goods which could be sold internationally. Indeed, he has suggested that regional economic configurations have emerged around the processing and export of staples. Certainly it could be argued after a review of the staple theorists that various population groupings emerged in North America in accordance with needs associated with the processing and/or export of staple commodities. Many present-day urban areas in Canada and the United States owe considerable credit to the needs of export staples for their positioning.

Although staples have played a very significant part in the economic history of North America and certain other jurisdictions, notably South Africa, Australia, and New Zealand, they should be viewed with caution as vehicles for the development of Third World economies. Growth and development based upon the exploitation of staples, where it was successful, was largely a nineteenth-century phenomenon. The demise of staples as dependable exports has been well explained (Nurkse, 1967). During the twentieth century the terms of trade have turned against staple commodities, thus rendering them questionable vehicles for economic expansion. Many parts of the Third World were heavily involved in supplying staple commodities to European nations. Unfortunately, such endeavors hardly prepared a foundation for growth or development in the jurisdictions concerned. Even in North America many of the regions which were most heavily involved in exporting staples are lagging in development.

The export of staples was a venture which mainly benefitted the exporter and various recipient nations. Those involved in such operations paid little attention to developing infrastructures which might be suitable for overall economic expansion. The major emphasis was generally placed upon port facilities, the sources of staples, and the transportation linkages that were needed to link the locations of the staples with the ports. Often, staple-producing areas tended to develop specialized infrastructures which were not readily suitable for the expansion of other activities. The emphasis upon port facilities causes population to expand, thus encouraging urban growth in those settings. As has been emphasized strongly in this book, population influxes cause the commitment of scarce public funds to the supply of urban services. In this case the forces at work tend to emphasize the needs of burgeoning seaports or other population concentrations that may develop at the locations of staple production.

In the case of various minerals and other staples which can become depleted over time, urban development in the areas surrounding them may result in a long-run drain of capital. If the mines run out, the raison d'être for certain settlements disappears. Facilities become abandoned and the infrastructure supporting the staple becomes redundant. A similar end is in store for facilities designed to facilitate the export of staple commodities which have become redundant or which have lost their markets.

It seems evident that economies which rely heavily upon export staples for their prosperity may be placing themselves in precarious positions. First of all, they may be facing terms of trade which are not in their favor. Second, they may develop infrastructures geared too heavily in the direction of staple exports. This will hardly aid them in encouraging economic integration or, for that matter, in encouraging the emergence of a viable national economy.

Third, in cases where undue interest in port facilities has been encouraged, the results may be population movements which create the need for major outlays for social overhead capital in those areas. To the extent that public funds are in short supply, such expenditures may force adjustments in priorities away from other significant developmental needs.

Unfortunately, the problems may not be limited to those enumerated above. As alluded to earlier, heavy outlays devoted to extractive activities generate expansion in mining and mineral processing towns which will result in serious losses should the mines be closed. In short, infrastructures constructed mainly to support primary production for export may well do serious damage to the efficient expansion of the national economy.

Even in the case where staple exports are continuing efficiently, problems seem unavoidable. The unfavorable nature of the terms of trade seems to encourage those who continue their involvement with staples to increase their output, where feasible, to make up for shortfalls in funds for needed imports. This they do by means of mechanization, which, of course, displaces workers, or by putting more land into the production of staples. The latter course of action may displace subsistence farmers or tenants of plantations who work the harvests in exchange for the use of small plots of land. The displacement of people from the land for whatever reason fuels the rural exodus and thus adds to the problems which urban areas are experiencing.

Of course, staple production for export may in many cases involve a trade-off with respect to food-stuffs for local consumption. Such a trade-off may at times necessitate the importing of food from abroad to feed the local population. Since much of what is imported will have been processed or packaged, it will of necessity carry with it comparative price differentials of the sort which stimulated trade problems with respect to the staple in the first place. Thus, the need to produce more staples for export of necessity increases the demand for processed food imports, thus further complicating the balance of trade. As urban populations grow in staple-exporting economies the need for food imports increases. Sound developmental planning would appear to suggest the utility of feeding local populations from local food sources where possible. Clearly, the type of import substitution that appears to be indicated constitutes a further argument against placing much emphasis on staple exports as a vehicle for development.

Dualism can also cause difficulties relating to economic integration in Third World jurisdictions. "In cases where a modern economy is superimposed in some manner upon a traditional one, developments with respect to the infrastructure are generally planned to accommodate the former" (McKee, 1977). Of course, there are strong arguments which appear to support such policy choices. If traditional means underdeveloped, few economists would recommend the allocation of funds to projects designed to sustain or perpetuate traditional economies. To do so would seem to support the contention that dualism is simply a stage in the process of development (Fei and Ranis, 1966). If such is the case, "the more pernicious aspects of it are merely short-run phenomena which must be ignored or endured if progress is to be sustained and long-term growth attained" (McKee, 1977).

Of course, it is a serious oversimplification to label dualism as a stage in the expansionary process. As has been suggested above, in dualistic societies it appears safe to assume that the modern economy or its needs will dictate the design of the infrastructure. This may mean actual pressure on governmental agencies or it may mean direct involvement of private interest groups. In either case, since there is little contact between the two economies, the traditional economy can expect minimum benefits from an infrastructure designed to service the modern economy (McKee, 1977). Since metropolitan areas tend to hold concentrations of modern sector activities it is hardly surprising when charges of urban bias surface. However, recognizing certain causal factors behind such charges hardly constitutes an endorsement.

An infrastructure designed to suit the needs of the modern sector will certainly reinforce disparities in welfare levels, while at the same time magnifying the gravitational pull of metropolitan complexes. Of course, it may also increase the gap between the modern and traditional economies. Since the bulk of the population will not be associated with the more advanced economy, the infrastructure cannot be expected to promote economic integration nationally. That being the case it will hardly support a truly viable expansion path for the economy as a whole. Following this logic it appears to be less than obvious that dualism is a stage in the development process. Certainly, it will perpetuate the gap between the two economies.

In cases where the bulk of modern sector activities is in the hands of foreign interests there may be an even greater danger. The infrastructure generated to meet the needs of modern activities will reflect business needs rather than the needs of the national economy. Thus, it would appear that policymakers would do well to avoid dualism wherever possible and to discourage it where it exists.

Although dualism was initially considered to be a social or cultural phenomenon (Boeke, 1953), the economic implications of it have been well studied. Dualism is known to be capable of reaching into the primary sector, thus merging certain difficulties discussed earlier with those being examined currently. An obvious example of this is the plantation economy. Plantation systems are based either upon a domestic aristocracy or some form of foreign ownership. This form of dualism has both social and economic implications. The plantation owners do well but the peasantry is shut out. Plantation economies are based mainly upon export and they develop infrastructures designed for that purpose. As suggested earlier, many plantation products are being impacted by unfavorable terms of trade. Beyond that problem, additional difficulties have arisen in some cases due to the introduction of synthetics and substitute products.

Thus, nations in the mold of what has been described above will find their modern sector or the activities most closely associated with the profit motive seriously weakened. Such nations are left with infrastructures supportive of staple exports which may not necessarily be capable of being switched to other pursuits. In Jamaica, for example, the export infrastructure designed to handle the bauxite trade is not positioned well to facilitate other economic initiatives in some cases. It appears as though a dualism which is based on staple exports can very well lead to economic stagnation in nations or regions which encounter it. On a policy level, it would appear that the agricultural sector should be encouraged to move toward supplying local needs if problems involving population drift and excessive urban expansion are to be contained. In other words, the production of primary products for export, however efficient in the execution, is hardly a safe developmental strategy.

Of course, forms of dualism can exist in which manufacturing activities are the base of the stronger of the two economies. In cases where the more modern economy revolves around manufacturing for export, an outward-looking infrastructure will emerge. In this configuration manufacturing units may have a tendency to locate near port facilities. Seaports and their hinterlands will prosper but other areas in the country may not. Manufacturing for export, nonetheless, has emerged as an effective growth strategy in recent years. Newly industrialized nations such as the Asian Tigers (Hong Kong, Singapore, South Korea, and Taiwan) have based their growth objectives on this option with apparent success. Despite such examples it should be noted that the outward-looking infrastructure needed to support manufacturing for export may militate against economic integration at the national level.

Although there are risks in adopting the strategy discussed above, when properly orchestrated it can generate positive returns. Unlike primary products, manufactured items need not anticipate unfavorable trading conditions in world markets. Foreign markets are available if the goods in question meet acceptable quality standards. Rather than contributing to difficulties with respect to trade balances, such goods will play a more positive role.

Difficulties may be inherent in the strategy if it implicitly accepts a dualism, whereby a traditional or subsistence economy is permitted to exist while export sectors are being encouraged. Almost by definition the existence of such a dualism implies the potential for growth without development, that is, a circumstance whereby more and more people are able to improve their material situations. If the export industries are highly capital intensive their ability to absorb labor will be limited. Such industries can often be justified by their positive impacts upon the balance of payments. A strategy which supports and encourages them may be better received and more conducive to development as well as growth if it is accompanied by encouragement for import substitution.

Import substitution is a desirable accompaniment to an export-oriented growth strategy for several reasons. It goes without saying that it should help the balance of payments. Beyond that, it should provide industrial employment opportunities which may begin to break down the dualism which seems to accompany the export strategy. Since the industries involved are by definition geared to local markets, they are less likely to feel the need to locate in ports or other locations geared to export. Thus, they may encourage the development of an infrastructure more conducive to economic integration. It seems likely as well that they will encourage the emergence of more employment opportunities because of the purchasing power acquired by their employees. Of course, they can strengthen their impacts in the domestic job market through using local materials where possible. The export industries accompanied by import substitution should contribute to both growth and development in ways that neither type of production might be able to do separately.

Of course, the emergence of manufacturing activities will strengthen the role of cities in the economies of emerging nations. Since urban settings are the most likely locational choices of production facilities, those areas will be making even more demands on public funds for the provision of infrastructure components and the urban services that industry will require. Although these circumstances will fuel the suspicions of those concerned with urban bias, they seem to be unavoidable components of a developmental strategy based upon industrialization. The degree to which such a strategy should be adopted or pursued must be evaluated on a case-by-case basis.

The industrialization strategy will require considerable attention on the part of the development planners. This is so not simply because of the major demands that production facilities will make on urban services and other forms of overhead capital, but also because their positioning and impact on urban complexes will have an overall bearing upon the development of urban configurations. Indeed, the positioning of manufacturing facilities is yet another element which, together with the location of new arrivals to the urban complex (Chapter 4) and the absorption of existing urban agglomerations (Chapter 5), must be considered if expanding urban mosaics are to be assured of continuing economic viability. Because of the important role which metropolitan complexes are playing in the expansion and viability of national economies, the nature and positioning of industrial units can hardly be ignored by planners at the national level.

Any discussion of dualism and the role of manufacturing activities in a developmental context must also consider the impact of

foreign manufacturing firms. There is hardly a shortage of literature concerning the advantages and disadvantages of multinational corporations. The current analysis will highlight the impact
that such enterprises have upon infrastructures and thus upon
development. One of the more serious issues related to foreign-
owned production facilities "is the global basis of decision making
which results in the tendency inherent in direct investment from
abroad to shift decision-making power in parts of the private sector
outside the country" (Parry, 1973). Such circumstances were recognized by proponents of pole theory. François Perroux, for example,
in considering the propulsive effects of industrial growth referred
to domination effects which might be experienced locally, region-
ally, nationally, or even internationally (Perroux, 1964).

Of course, decisions on the part of multinational firms to establish production facilities in Third World nations are made in keeping with the perceptions of corporate planners. Such decisions are
multifaceted. They may involve a desire to cut labor costs in
operations that require minimal skill. They may also result from a
search for cheaper resource inputs. In some cases firms may locate
in Third World settings with ambitions of accessing local markets.
In other cases firms elect Third World settings to minimize taxes
and/or government regulatory interventions. Beyond those considerations they may be seeking concessions on energy or water
use or other forms of support which governments may offer. Such
support systems may even reach as far as the use of public funds
to supply specific adjustments in infrastructure components, in
keeping with the stated needs of the firms in question. It seems
clear that governments contemplating the hosting of multinational
manufacturing facilities should weigh the potential impacts carefully as part of their planning procedures (McKee, 1991a, 48).

"Since the international firms are pursuing their own interests
and are only peripherally concerned with the welfare of specific
countries, any influence which they may have . . . will affect their
own needs and not necessarily those of the country concerned"
(McKee, 1977). Perroux stated the case very succinctly when he
suggested that such enterprises "create durable, structural spaces
within economic and territorial systems" (1988, 52). Such perceptions seem especially accurate with respect to the emergence of an
infrastructure.

Jean Paelinck has suggested the impact which a dominant enterprise can assert upon economic relationships within a region (1965, 10, 11). Of course, he was for the most part concerned with relations within the private sector, rather than multinational firms in particular, but his perceptions seem easy to apply. "[T]he multinational firm is a center of economic, technological, financial and parapolitical power" (Bocage, 1985, 160). Firms which hold such power may very well assert undue influence upon the development of infrastructure components. If the results of such influence coincide with the goals or understood needs of the economy in question, this is no more than a happy accident. It seems more probable that the infrastructure will reflect the needs of the firms in question as they pursue their corporate objectives.

Since the types of production facilities in question will most probably be urban based, the infrastructure specified may impact the physical structure of cities or metropolitan areas. Remembering that foreign-owned production facilities will function in accordance with the needs of their firms in world markets, not to mention the level of ongoing success which those firms enjoy, the prominence of such production facilities raises uncertainties for their hosts. Urban areas which become heavily dependent on such enterprises may find themselves in even more serious difficulties than the demise of the production units may imply. "Beyond the losses engendered by the activities themselves are impacts from resource immobilities and rigidities in the infrastructure" (McKee, 1991a). Thus, accommodations that were made to the needs of foreign manufacturing units may become barriers to needed patterns of change, should the user units become defunct. Of course, domestic enterprises can fail as well, leaving inopportune rigidities in their wake. However, in the case of multinational firms, the level of uncertainty is raised.

It seems quite clear that "Those charged with planning the infrastructures of developing nations must be able to predict the future of private enterprise" (McKee, 1977). This is very important in metropolitan complexes where planners not only need to know the ongoing needs of industrial units vis-à-vis the urban infrastructure components, but must also plan for where industry should be positioned physically. Without such planning, efficiency in metropolitan complexes may be difficult to realize, much less sustain.

Such detail with respect to the actual or planned direction of corporate activity is difficult to obtain if the industrial decision makers are native to the jurisdictions concerned. It may be more difficult if they are foreign yet resident in the territories in which they operate, and it may be impossible if they are not resident. It is known that this difficulty with respect to multinational firms can precipitate the "erosion of national economic and political sovereignty" because such enterprises can "circumvent national economic policies" and their concerns within specific nations are frequently supported by the governments of their parent nations (Parry, 1973).

It seems clear that the impacts which foreign firms may have upon the infrastructures of Third World host nations will depend upon whether their primary operations are directed toward domestic markets or exports. Where the firms are seeking to penetrate domestic markets the results may be beneficial, as in the case of import substitution in general. Unfortunately, many Third World nations are rather small in terms of population and thus may not be good targets for import substitution practiced by foreign firms. Writing on that general subject, G. K. Helleiner has suggested that "since the opportunity for efficient import-substituting industrialization is exhausted rather quickly," there is little opportunity for establishing an industrial mix that is not geared toward exports (1973). Indeed, with considerable foresight he labeled manufacturing for export as the new frontier for international business in what has been depicted as the Third World (1973). Clearly, the planners should be active if they hope to ensure that urban and even national infrastructures meet domestic as well as export needs. Beyond that, they must provide for the flexibility to meet changing developmental needs as the industrial mix changes, as it most assuredly will (McKee, 1991a).

In the current chapter various situations have been highlighted which may tend to slant Third World economies toward international relationships and commitments. Since most of these economies have developed urban orientations, ongoing flexibility has emerged as a serious issue. Since outward-looking activities require outward-looking infrastructures, the needs of national economic integration and perhaps even diversification may be poorly served. Such economies may not develop the type of independence normally associated with nation states. Of course, in the international economy as it exists today, independence as it was traditionally understood may be largely moot. Nonetheless, planners can assure that domestic needs are served by more careful attention to how the components of the infrastructure are chosen and placed and how they can be changed or expanded. Such attention seems especially pertinent in metropolitan settings.

8

The Impact of Tourism

The advances in transportation and communications which have occurred during the second half of the twentieth century have brought with them many dramatic adjustments in the makeup of the global economy. Among the most dramatic of these changes has been the emergence of a variety of industries which are truly international in scope. Firms within many manufacturing industries have extended their production processes into numerous jurisdictions throughout the world. Less-visible service industries have followed suit with the intention of fulfilling the needs of their production-oriented customers. Parallel to these developments has been the emergence of an international service conglomerate which, if considered as an industry, would undoubtedly be one of the largest and fastest growing in the international economy. The industry in question is international tourism.

Space does not permit a general overview of that industry and how it came to be. The concern here will be the role which tourism plays in urban settings in emerging nations and how that role impacts the processes of development both locally and nationally. In advanced nations tourism has been a boon to local and regional development in some cases. In the United States no one would dispute the impact of tourism in an Orlando or a Las Vegas. In this country urban centers which owe their continuing economic strength in large part to leisure-time activities abound. With such visible successes in the United States and other developed nations it is hardly surprising that various Third World nations are looking to tourism as a potential contributor to their development ambitions. As would be the case with any industry which Third World jurisdictions might contemplate hosting, advance planning is advisable. This is especially true if the nation in question is intending to establish major tourist facilities in urban settings.

International tourism has been described as "a large and complicated mix of businesses in transportation and communications, entertainment and recreation, food and lodging and support services" (McKee, 1988, 122). Clearly, Third World jurisdictions aspiring to host tourist facilities must invest in a transportation and communications infrastructure which can deliver the tourists and service their needs. Since transportation and communications components tend to be located so as to service existing urban areas or, more specifically, their need for external linkages, it is hardly surprising when the advent of tourism reinforces the strength of those infrastructure components and with them the urban emphasis in the host economy.

The international tourism industry "is in the business of providing a wide range of consumer services, differentiated by destination as well as by activities, to customers wishing to purchase vacations" (McKee, 1988, 122). It has grown in size and scope to the point where few locations remain inaccessible to the international traveler. Of course, Himalayan expeditions or treks to the innermost sanctuaries of the Amazon rain forest are not a part of the present context. The concern here is for the less sophisticated, mass production segments of the touring public, their service providers, and their impact on Third World urban settings.

Economists appear to be in accord that the main reasons why specific Third World jurisdictions may find it attractive to host significant numbers of foreign visitors revolve around the potential for providing domestic employment opportunities while at the same time bettering their foreign exchange positions. From the point of view of host governments, the case for mass tourism is strong or weak depending upon the potential for realizing either or both of those stated goals.

Beyond those goals, decisions involving the expansion of tourism must also involve the potential impact that the industry may have upon the local culture and environment, resource utilization, and the general quality of life. Because the advantages of economies of scale with respect to mass tourism appear to dictate the concentration of both facilities and infrastructure, it appears as though the answers to issues raised here are best sought against an urban backdrop. Since urban environments are most conducive to mass tourism, they will incur the most visible and lasting impacts from it. Thus, tourism in those environments must be examined from the point of view of how it impacts general developmental aims.

Tourists actually purchase "rights of access to public goods such as beaches, parks or police protection . . . [and] the services of public utilities, such as clean water and electricity" (Tucker and Sundberg, 1988, 145). Tucker and Sundberg go on to suggest that expenditure patterns are what determine the impact of tourism in specific locations. If this is true, development planners should be concerned with channeling those expenditure patterns in directions that support their overall developmental goals and away from incursions which thwart or revise those goals. Tucker and Sundberg feel that the number of visitors is a less useful concept "than measures of the magnitude of expenditures and their subsequent impact on the growth and development of the host economy or region" (146). Implicit in this observation is the idea that expenditures on the part of tourists are much more important to host nations than the generation of massive traffic. Thus, planners may be well advised to exercise caution with respect to the uncontrolled expansion of tourist capacity.

Even host jurisdictions which are enjoying obvious financial benefits from tourism should exercise caution with regard to the uncontrolled expansion of the industry. Hard lessons have been learned in wealthier nations where too much confidence was placed in particular industries, however robust those industries may have appeared. Declining fortunes in particular industries have left manufacturing centers and indeed entire regions in crisis. Economists are generally in agreement that diversification provides a certain amount of insulation from the downside risks of industrial change. In Third World settings diversification should be an important concern for the planners.

"In opting to encourage tourism as part of their developmental strategies Third World nations should be careful to allow for economic diversification" (Mamoozadeh and McKee, 1990, 155). Since tourism is basically an international industry, by relying too heavily upon it Third World settings increase their dependence upon events beyond their control. "Jurisdictions which become overbalanced toward tourism may suffer negative impacts from recessions in economies from which their customers emanate" (1990). In addition to recessions beyond their shores or changes in currency values, not to mention international political or military difficulties (all of which are well beyond the control of specific host nations), there are potential difficulties within the industry itself. The rise of competing destinations, changing tastes among tourists, or new goals or emphases among multinational firms which are components of the tourism conglomerate may alter the fortunes of specific host jurisdictions irreparably.

The uncertainties referred to above have clear implications for Third World urban centers. Such centers may undergo substantial physical adjustments, prompted by the needs of the tourist industry. The creation of an infrastructure geared toward tourism may cause reduced priorities to be placed on legitimate local needs. Such adjustments may be most obvious among nations which are both small and poor. Among such jurisdictions various public services may be truncated in scope in order to provide public funds for tourist-oriented infrastructure adjustments. Further priority adjustments may be made to ensure the supply of water, energy, and other resource requirements to hotels and other facilities geared toward tourism. In extreme cases tourism can cause dramatic alterations in the physical plans of urban areas as well as the positioning of other activities within them. The costs can only be measured in potential economic activities foregone and, of course, in inconvenience and/or costs to local residents. In cases where the urban centers in question form the base for the national economy the costs of national goal adjustments must also be considered.

All of the considerations enumerated in the preceding paragraph should be of concern in jurisdictions where tourism appears to be an ongoing success. If circumstances beyond the control of host nations conspire to cause difficulties for the tourist ventures, those difficulties become immediately evident in the urban settings where tourist facilities are positioned. If the tourists stop coming or even if they arrive in reduced numbers the impact is immediate and unpleasant. Of course, the tourist spigot may be turned off by local difficulties as well as international considerations—witness Jamaica in the late 1970s.

Those who have witnessed plant closings or industrial retrenchment in advanced nations can readily imagine the impact in urban settings. If the tourists are suddenly absent, hotels shut down and various support and entertainment facilities are at risk. The suprastructure of tourism, meaning the shops and restaurants, the hotels, and other facilities occupy space in impacted urban complexes. The absence of tourists serves to highlight the negative aspects of these circumstances—the inflexibility of physical capital once it is in place. In the absence of tourists the anticipated positive contributions to foreign exchange and many of the tourist-related employment opportunities dry up. The tourist facilities, if they are to remain usable, require maintenance. Many such facilities may have no immediate secondary uses. They are simply there, they occupy space, and they are subject to deterioration.

If it seems that such downside risks have more negative potential in urban environments it might seem logical for development planners in emerging nations to locate tourist facilities away from urban complexes. In the case of facilities geared to mass tourism this may not be feasible. It is the urban areas that have the transportation and communications linkages that make mass tourism feasible. Observations made elsewhere with respect to small island nations may apply in the present context. Major gateways to Third World nations, for example, airports and harbors, tend to be in or near major urban areas (McKee and Tisdell, 1990, 51). "Entry and departure formalities are frequently centralized at such points, and the international transport industry draws on services and inputs that usually can be provided only in or near a large urban center" (51).

The consumer side of mass tourism may tend to keep the tourists in or near the large urban centers in question. "The further a tourist moves beyond his or her point of entry to a country, the greater is the cost and the time required" (McKee and Tisdell, 1990, 51). Although there are exceptions, it would appear that mass tourism involving charter flights and junkets of a few days or a week almost presuppose that the visitors are housed in or near urban areas. In such settings economies of scale in servicing visitors may be most easily realized. Such settings may also reassure potential visitors that contemplated trips are not too adventurous, an assurance that may be deemed necessary if the industry is to maintain an acceptable throughput of clients.

It has been recognized that tourists often expect facilities that are only to be found in urban environments (McKee and Tisdell, 1990, 51). Included in such expectations are ranges of shopping facilities, easy access to medical and related services, communications with their homes, and various other entertainment and cultural activities. Although nonurban tourist enclaves do exist in Third World settings (McKee, 1988) those are hardly the focus here. It seems clear that mass tourism is dependent largely upon urban settings. The issue here is under what circumstances and to what extent the industry can be beneficial to host jurisdictions. For the planners the issue relates to trade-offs between the overall economic efficiency of urban complexes and the needs of the tourist industry. In Third World settings tourism of the urban variety must be considered in terms of what it does for overall development goals.

As stated earlier, the two most important justifications for the hosting of tourist facilities in Third World settings are that it assists the balance of payments through the earning of foreign exchange and that it provides jobs. In the case of the first objective it has been suggested that attention should be given to the reduction of the import content of tourist expenditures (Palmer, 1979, 131). Whether or not mass tourism in an urban setting can achieve the result advocated by Palmer must be examined on a case-by-case basis. It is possible that certain items needed by mass tourism can be produced locally, provided that needed know-how and raw materials are available. Unfortunately, it is also possible that the economies of supply may dictate the importing of various items. In this last case local production, where it exists, may be reduced or eliminated. Of course, demonstration effects, among the local population which are undoubtedly intensified in urban settings, may increase the demand for items imported for the use of tourists.

Certainly, mass tourism directed toward urban areas creates jobs. The benefit from this depends upon the skill level of the jobs created, the pay scale, and who fills the job openings. If foreigners are imported to staff the skilled, higher-paying positions while local workers are relegated to menial pursuits, the positive impact may be lessened. Even low-paying employment opportunities, if they exist in sufficient numbers, may encourage in-migration to the urban areas in question. The impact of this on the local economy must be studied on a case-by-case basis, although it would appear that impacts may be proportionately more significant in smaller and poorer jurisdictions. In cases where urban expansion is driven by tourism, and where local residents by and large are confined to menial, low-paying jobs related to it and where the industry increases the dependence of the local economy on imports, a recipe for major problems is possibly being written.

Among tourists, those who settle for mass-marketed packages and destinations are the bargain-hunters of the industry. Although they may be wealthy by Third World standards, they hardly fit the jet-set image, nor are they the current prototypes of the travelers who appeared in remote or challenging settings earlier in this century. Robert Reich has suggested that "one of the attractions of a vacation on a Caribbean island, the Mexican Gulf coast, or Baja California, by contrast with Miami Beach or San Diego is that in-person service can be had in the former regions for a fraction of the cost in the latter" (1992, 298). In other words, the expansion of mass tourism in Third World settings is possibly being driven by the same engine that has been driving the expansion of the production facilities of multinational firms in similar settings.

Concentrations of tourist facilities may be emerging in Third World urban complexes to take advantage of cheaper labor and operating costs. Such enclaves are hardly vacation options considered by upscale travelers. They rely for their ongoing success and profitability upon mass marketing and advertising, aimed at the tourists who pay for their junkets in lump sums before they leave their homes. After the international airlines and the hotel chains receive their shares, little may be left to augment host economies directly. The question becomes how much will such visitors spend in Third World settings beyond their prepaid package fee, and what will be the impact of the facilities that they occupy upon host economies. In many cases per diem expenditures may be less than those incurred by cruise ship passengers, which may well be minimal. In other words, the type of tourism under discussion operates under supermarket conditions, where financial success in host jurisdictions relies upon massive customer quotas. This dictates large hotels and large outlays on the infrastructure required to maintain acceptable occupancy rates.

If benefits for host jurisdictions seem tenuous at this point in the discussion, the search for a justification for mass tourism in Third World urban complexes must be extended. Habibullah Khan, Chou Fee Seng, and Wong Kwei Cheong have suggested that, beyond what has been considered here, tourism generates additional government revenue and promotes economic development through various multiplier effects (1988, 132). Those authors acknowledge that tourism raises revenues through airport taxes and hotel tariffs as well as through indirect taxes charged on various goods and services which tourists consume. However, they realize that various public expenditures may negate those revenues and suggest that it is "difficult to determine the net revenue earned by the government through tourism-related projects since these facilities are also used by local residents" (134).

Perhaps net public revenue gains from tourism may not be required to justify the industry. If revenues attributable to tourism pay for infrastructure improvements which benefit the local economy, tourism has made a positive contribution. Of course, negative contributions are also possible where revenues are used to extend infrastructure components to facilitate tourism in ways which are detrimental to other domestic considerations. In the Bahamas, for example, additions to cruise ship dockage space in Nassau have made the harbor a much less flexible facility. The provision of water, electricity, and other services to major tourist facilities in urban areas where such services are in short supply would be another example. On the positive side, local residents may benefit if they are able to share in public services and recreational facilities developed to facilitate tourism. Clearly, the extension of infrastructure components and public services should be given careful attention by the planners and should rarely be dictated by ad hoc demands from the tourist sector.

Earlier in this volume it was suggested that squatter settlements should receive the attention of the planners in terms of their positioning in urban areas and also in terms of which public services they should receive. Surely a similar prescription should be written for tourist facilities. In very large Third World metropolitan areas mass tourism may not reach the level where its positioning impacts the physical structure and functioning of the urban complex. Certainly, concentrations of tourist-related facilities can be identified in centers like Mexico City and Rio de Janeiro, but no one would suggest that such concentrations are impeding the functioning of the economies of those complexes. In such settings tourism is simply another industry which adds to their economic diversity. Of course, this is not to suggest that tourism or, more specifically, the positioning of tourist facilities should be given carte blanche in such settings or that it should take precedence over local needs or preclude local residents' needed services or access to recreational areas.

In major Third World metropolitan areas mass tourism may be best able to promote economic development through the multiplier effects referred to by Khan, Seng, and Cheong (1988, 132). Expanding tourist facilities in such settings may broaden the market for domestic production. This is not simply due to direct purchases by tourists. "Jobs will be created in industries supplying hotel and resort furnishings; athletic equipment of various sorts . . . and domestically produced food" (McKee, 1988, 45). Obviously, such demands will have both income and employment effects which are well known to economists. Local suppliers of building materials, not to mention actual construction firms, should benefit from ongoing tourist expansion. Those concerned with maximizing the positive impact from tourism in such settings should concern themselves with the positioning of facilities and should encourage the use of local goods and services.

Positive impacts from tourism may be more difficult to generate and maintain in smaller nations and, of course, in smaller urban complexes. In smaller nations it is less likely that multiplier effects from tourism will be as strong in the domestic economy. The resources and skilled labor may not be available, thus necessitating increases in imports of goods such as those referred to in the preceding paragraph. Foreign engineers and construction contractors may have to be employed. Public services needed to support tourism may have proportionately greater impacts on domestic priorities. In such settings it appears as though the planners should be even more watchful.

Smaller cities which are the loci of modern sector endeavors in various Third World settings can be permanently impacted in dramatic ways by an overlay of enterprises geared to mass tourism. Examples have become obvious in the Caribbean Basin region. The small, independent nations in that area are natural hosts for mass tourism. Not only do they have the climate and recreational opportunities which many vacationers seek, they also enjoy relatively easy access from the major population centers of North America.

The Bahamas on the northern periphery of the Caribbean Basin region affords an excellent example of how mass tourism can impact an urban setting. Since its independence in 1973 the nation has been moving ever more strongly toward becoming a major tourist mecca. Although it boasts some 700 islands, relatively few are inhabited, and more than two-thirds of its population of fewer than 300,000 persons reside on the island of New Providence, which houses its capital and principal city, Nassau.

Throughout the 1980s the Bahamas opted for mass tourism as a vehicle for economic expansion. During that period airports and port facilities underwent major expansion. On the Island of New Providence massive new hotels were built. Facilities on Paradise Island, which is adjacent, were enlarged as well. "New Providence and Paradise Island accommodations range from plush suites and seaside cottages to bath sharing guest rooms. In all there are seventy-three hotels (totalling 7,810 rooms) to choose from" (*Bahamas Handbook*, 1991, 226). As mentioned earlier, cruise ship capacity has been greatly extended in Nassau. A recent visit by the author to that city coincided with the arrival of fourteen cruise ships which were carrying 10,000 travel agents for a five-day convention. Tourism officials were of the opinion that the invasion of travel agents via cruise ships might net them a half-billion dollars worth of future land-based business. The accuracy of their hopes or predictions remains to be seen.

By opting for mass tourism and providing the infrastructure and suprastructure to support it the Bahamas has placed itself in the position of having to deliver a continually large and perhaps increasing nose count. Anything less than that might result in hotel and restaurant closures, idle tourist-related service personnel, and economic malaise. If events beyond its shores should impact tourist arrivals it may be powerless to avoid rapid economic fallout.

Although international tourism is a growing industry it is not without risk to specific jurisdictions, due to its reliance upon a foreign clientele. Coupled with that is the fact that tourist facilities are not readily transferable to other pursuits, meaning that a drop in demand may result in large sunk costs. The advent of new facilities may render existing hotels less attractive by comparison, thus resulting in declining occupancy rates. In regions like the Caribbean, international competition may drive continuing expenditures on the upgrading of facilities as well as the building of new ones. In some destinations this may impose an increasing cost framework upon the industry at the same time that the need to maintain acceptable throughputs results in price cutting.

As suggested before, by opting for large numbers of visitors, Third World economies are following the commercial example set by supermarkets and discount stores. The scale of business is designed to ensure success on small profit margins. The mass marketing that such an approach requires may drive upscale tourists away. Large-scale facilities are more likely to be the preserve of multinational firms which may mean less scope for local operators. Mass tourism means more area devoted to hotels and resorts and more local resources and services slanted in that direction. In smaller urban settings such overlays can certainly impair the efficiency of the local economy, not to mention slanting it irreparably in the direction of tourism.

Not to belabor what has occurred in the Bahamas it must be said that Nassau today is a very different urban center than it was prior to the advent of mass tourism. Prior to independence Nassau was the capital of the colony and a destination for upscale vacationers. Two of the major hotels from that era stand empty today, rather obvious casualties of an expanding mass-marketed tourist sector. Many governmental functions are still housed in colonial buildings at the center of the city and an overlay of banks is apparent. Beyond that the changes are dramatic.

More than half of the stores and commercial establishments in the center of the city are geared to the tourist trade. These range from a major straw market and outlets for imported souvenirs and artifacts to stores selling top-of-the-line luxury items. What appears to be the major shopping area for local residents is at some distance from the central business district and not very accessible to those without automobiles. In other words, local economic activity is being relocated to facilitate tourist-oriented business. The harbor has undergone functional realignments to facilitate increased cruise ship traffic. The city with street patterns predating the automobile is noticeably congested.

Tourism in Nassau and more generally in New Providence has been discussed elsewhere (McKee, 1988, 48ff). "There have been obvious benefits . . . but in the course of pursuing them the island and its infrastructure has been greatly changed" (48). Large resorts have placed pressure upon local transportation facilities and the power supply. Water is not plentiful and large quantities of it are brought in from Andros, a larger island some miles away. Tourism has clearly been given priority by the government. The problem is the inflexibility that such massive developments have brought with them.

Evidence of similar developmental priorities can be found in various jurisdictions throughout the Caribbean region. Each destination in the region is in competition with the remainder and all are in competition with the fleet of cruise ships which is growing in number as well as in the size of vessels. The Caribbean region may be in a stronger position with respect to the potential of tourism as compared to various other Third World jurisdictions. Despite that, painful lessons are being learned which need not be relearned elsewhere.

The real or imagined problems being experienced in the Caribbean are no reason for Third World nations to avoid tourism in its entirety. If tooling up for tourism brings with it an infrastructure which is better able to serve local needs, that is all to the good. No one would argue that the industry fails to generate employment or that it holds no potential for earning foreign exchange. It can bring very real benefits to Third World locations. Yet the planners should realize that the caution flags are flying. "If . . . the provision of the infrastructure for tourism does not extend benefits to the local people, or if it creates negative externalities, then it actually becomes an obstacle to the orderly expansion of the economy" (McKee, 1988, 50).

It must be remembered that urban settings in Third World nations are the most likely locations for major tourist facilities. Since those settings are also the locations of choice for the bulk of modern sector activities they are the locus of growth in Third World economies. When tourism begins to interfere with growth and development in those urban settings it seems logical to assume that it has either surpassed its optimum limits or its components are poorly located or mismanaged. For host economies the object is hardly to maximize the number of visitors but rather to maximize the benefits which can be gained from visitors.

Urban areas and Third World settings in general may be better served by hosting smaller numbers of upscale visitors. This reduces demands upon the infrastructure and local services, not to mention the environment. It reduces the danger of acquiring an oversupply of inflexible facilities. At the same time it does create some jobs and may earn some foreign exchange. Beyond that, smaller facilities for upscale visitors may be within the capacity of local business interests to develop. Where this form of tourism is developed the benefits remain with the local economy rather than being syphoned off by large, multinational resort chains. Upscale tourist facilities are less at risk from downturns in the international economy. Patrons will pay a premium for the less-frenetic atmosphere of smaller, less-crowded resorts. Since the facilities are small, less mass marketing is needed nor do fire sale prices seem as necessary. The logic here should hardly be construed as elitist. Tourism in Third World locations is hardly about class but rather about contributing positively to growth and development.

9

The Urban Role in Small Economies

Much of the literature on issues related to urbanization in emerging nations pertains to the emergence of very large cities and what that phenomenon portends for development. In many Third World jurisdictions the megacity issue hardly pertains, since they do not possess the population to generate such complexes. As many as eighty jurisdictions have populations of ten million or less with many boasting fewer than one million inhabitants. In such economies the major problem may be thought to be critical mass rather than urbanization. There is no doubt that many independent nations are limited by the size of their human resource base, but even among the smallest jurisdictions urbanization can be fraught with problems.

Since the modern sectors of most economies are urban based it is to be expected that those economies will have to rely upon urban environments to provide the foundation for development. A recent discussion of urbanization in small island nations suggested that such jurisdictions "may be experiencing problems related to urbanization, similar in nature, if not in extent, to those that have been documented in larger emerging nations" (McKee and Tisdell, 1990, 59). It seems reasonable to suggest that this observation could be broadened to include most small emerging nations.

Urban places become obstacles to development if the rigidities of their form interfere with economic change and the needs of businesses which they house. Unfortunately, such issues can emerge in rather small urban complexes. In small economies difficulties associated with cities can translate very quickly into difficulties at the national level. Indeed, some small economies are virtual city-states to begin with. In such settings urban rigidities which impact economic change must be high on the priority lists of those concerned with growth and development. The most obvious examples of small emerging nations which are virtual city-states would be Hong Kong and Singapore. Their entire populations have been listed as resident in their respective largest cities (United Nations, 1991, 158).

The same United Nations document listed seventeen other nations with at least 90 percent of their populations housed in single urban places. Clearly, the national growth and development of such jurisdictions is inextricably linked to circumstances in their major urban centers. Some such urban complexes are rather sizable. "In the Caribbean region alone Havana, San Juan and Santo Domingo would have to be considered as major metropolitan areas by any reasonable standard" (McKee and Tisdell, 1990, 60). Kingston is approaching that status as well. Metropolitan areas such as those cited here will never reach the scale of various Latin American centers often alluded to in the literature on development, but without a doubt they are having major impacts upon the nations which house them. As a consequence they and others like them deserve the attention of development planners.

In small nations the shift in emphasis from agriculture to secondary and tertiary pursuits may impact migration patterns more dramatically than has been the case in larger emerging nations. The same can be said of the increased mechanization of agriculture or even an increasing emphasis on export crops. Secondary and tertiary modern sector activities do tend to be urban based in small emerging nations, but they may be very different in nature and impact from what has come to be recognized as reality in larger Third World economies.

Many smaller Third World nations were formerly controlled by various wealthier states. In many of those jurisdictions the principal urban complex housed various governmental and administrative functions during the period of foreign domination. Often the infrastructure and even the design of such urban complexes were tailored to meet the needs of a colonial administration. In the case of small island nations it has been suggested that "these centers also served various functions relating to transportation and communications in as much as linkages were required with the external world" (McKee and Tisdell, 1990, 61). There is little reason to suspect that administrative centers in mainland ministates performed vastly different functions. In many smaller Third World nations the principal urban complex is still constrained by structural and physical rigidities dating from the colonial era. If such complexes are to be reliable locations for growth-oriented activities they require the careful attention of planners.

Of course, the administrative functions of such complexes have hardly been curtailed by the severing of formal links with wealthier nations. If anything the public functions which they house have increased as they have become the seats of government for independent nations. Indeed, the involvement of the labor force in governmental activities is proportionately much more substantial in smaller nations than is the case with larger jurisdictions. The establishment of independent nations appears to justify if not necessitate the establishment of rather extensive cadres of ministries, bureaus, and quasi-public agencies. The staffing of such organizations has a substantial impact upon the complexion of the labor force in nations where modern sector opportunities in the private sector may be less than extensive. Beyond this there is the tendency common to many Third World nations to permit, if not encourage, the expansion of governmental bureaucracies in the face of serious unemployment problems.

Since governmental agencies tend to be housed in urban environments, their expansion causes the urban complexes in question to expand. Since this scenario in small nations means the expansion of capital cities it also means that those urban complexes will develop a suprastructure and infrastructure which facilitates government functions. Whether or not private sector initiatives are encouraged or impeded by such developments must be considered on a case-by-case basis. In their deliberations the planners must consider that their capitals are the most likely settings for any private sector expansion that may be contemplated.

Since civil service employment provides a relatively attractive source of income in small Third World nations, it has become a career path for some who may have considered professional careers as an alternative. In many jurisdictions a relatively well-off class of civil servants has emerged, the members of which enjoy a standard of living that would compare favorably to those in white-collar, middle-income elements in the populations of wealthier nations. Since this class is urban based it will have an impact upon urban environments which goes beyond the impact of the government agencies in which its members are employed.

Its most visible impacts will be in the domestic sector of the urban economy and in the urban services and infrastructure needed to support that sector. Beyond these influences, this relatively affluent, urbanized population supported by public sector employment will have significant induced investment impacts upon the economies of the nations concerned. These impacts may be visible most immediately in private sector consumer services.

In the case of wealthier nations, services have often been considered to be less desirable than secondary pursuits by those concerned with the continued viability of the economies in question (see Cohen and Zysman, 1987). "In a Keynesian sense many service endeavors geared towards consumers are perceived by economists to be induced activities, presumably generated in urban areas because of a successful manufacturing base" (McKee, 1988, 112). Such a view of consumer services understates their importance in the urban complexes of small, emerging nations. It is true that they may not be generated by income earned in manufacturing but their paternity is hardly the significant issue. Although the demand for them may originate in income earned from public service and, of course, from well-recognized consumer service needs occasioned by urban living, they do provide job opportunities of varying skill requirements and by doing so they expand the modern sectors of the economies in question.

As has been postulated elsewhere with respect to small island nations, "a major impact of the public service sector . . . has been to foster urbanization and centralization of economic activity" (McKee and Tisdell, 1990, 45). Urban economic expansion, stemming from the primary impact of the public sector combined with secondary impacts from consumer services, acts as a draw for rural populations who may see a better future in such pursuits than what they can look forward to in agriculture and other forms of primary production.

In many smaller emerging nations a move to the city may not seem as threatening as in cases where it entails the cutting of rural ties in favor of a future among the teeming informal sectors of megacities. This is especially true in very small jurisdictions where such a move need not cut ties with the countryside. Some such economies are approaching the status of city-states. Examples of such configurations are relatively common in the Caribbean basin. In such economies urban centers afford entry-level employment opportunities in various consumer service industries. In some cases aspirants to such work opportunities are urban residents, while in other instances workers commute to work through the use of minibusses or route taxies. The citizens of such jurisdictions tend to identify ever more closely over time with urban life-styles, thus reinforcing the reality of the urban ministate.

In such jurisdictions, development planners on the domestic level must ensure the continuing viability of the urban environment as a climate where modern sector activities can flourish. This means that they must ensure that an influx of new urban residents does not render the physical infrastructure of the city unworkable, while at the same time ensuring that the nonurban areas of the nations in question are not cut off from a share of the benefits from development. In states which are small geographically and dominated by their capital cities, the planners must focus on an efficient urban environment while at the same time ensuring economic integration by developing infrastructure components and various services on a national level.

If educational opportunities on a national scale are geared to providing what is needed for survival in an urban environment, there will be better assurances that surplus labor will be absorbed and that expansion will not be curtailed by an influx of the unemployable to the city. Good transportation linkages to the city, together with a communications infrastructure and the provision of electrical service on a nationwide basis will improve economic integration, strengthen the economy, and at the same time make it less necessary for rural population to move to the city. In its most optimistic format such a planning scenario should reduce urban overcrowding involving slums and squatter settlements by raising rural living standards and providing rural residents access to urban labor markets and services.

Even in such very small jurisdictions, where government service appears to be one of the linchpins of the economy, the forces of urbanization do generate economic difficulties for development planners. In the Caribbean, for example, some jurisdictions which are independent today had their economic origins as plantation colonies of European nations. Today, as independent nations, some such territories are finding the transition from an economy based upon primary exports to one based upon services rather painful. An urban economy of any significant size necessitates supplying the food needs of a population employed in urban pursuits. Small independent nations are generally well advised to provide as much of their food needs as possible from domestic sources. In cases where agricultural land is given over to export crops adjustments are indicated. Indeed, Third World nations of any size may be well advised to practice import substitution with respect to food where possible, in order to reduce difficulties with respect to the balance of payments.

Nations which are small in both population and land area may still be able to derive some benefit from such policies. Foodstuffs are not the only items which cause balance of payments difficulties for smaller nations. Almost by definition such economies lack the critical mass to generate adequate markets for domestic manufacturing ventures. Certainly small nations are faced with the necessity of importing the bulk of needed consumer durables and indeed a wide variety of manufactured products which larger nations may opt to produce domestically. As a consequence, balance of payments difficulties may easily interfere with the development prospects of small Third World nations.

In circumventing such difficulties the theoretical possibilities include reducing imports and/or increasing exports. Import reduction implies that some imports are nonessential and thus can be reduced by government action, or that a general cutback in imports can be accomplished through government action or moral suasion, or that nations can produce more of their needs locally or substitute other locally supplied products for particular imports. The above appears to be a logical taxonomy of procedures which might be applied individually or in consort to meet the needs of specific economies. Their impact on small, urban-based economies requires more elaboration.

Small economies that are urban based may be faced with a dichotomy when it comes to dealing with imports. It seems clear that they would strengthen their economic positions by cutting down on imports. Doing so would, as already suggested, strengthen their balance of trade position but it would also protect them from cyclical pressures in the world economy which might reach their domestic economies through the vehicle of imports. Limiting imports in some fashion may allow a certain amount of domestic production to develop, limited, of course, by the size of the economies in question. As already suggested, an import substitution strategy may not be usable on a wide scale. Nonetheless, it could be employed in many jurisdictions in the case of foodstuffs, clothing, and other items conducive to small-scale production for domestic markets.

The dichotomous relationship with respect to imports emerges in the case of urban-based economies. Despite the logic of limiting imports, urban settings will require the use of numerous manufactured products which cannot be supplied locally. Not only will these products have to be imported, the demand for them will grow with the size of urban complexes. Thus, growth and change in urban complexes will increase the dependence upon imports. It seems evident that successful development may be unattainable. Therefore, the planners will have to balance the damage which imports may inflict against a very real need for them.

In many Third World settings problems related to terms of trade may be exacerbated by increasing exports rather than relying upon import reductions. There are cases where small nations have included manufacturing for export as a part of their developmental strategies. Hong Kong and Singapore have been rather successful in that regard. In addition to needed foreign exchange earnings such a practice provides domestic employment, and if products can be marketed domestically, may also reduce the need for imports.

Unfortunately, many small Third World nations may be unable to sustain a developmental strategy based upon manufacturing for export. The reasons for this are well beyond the parameters of the present project. Suffice it to say that in cases where manufacturing for export is feasible, production facilities will tend to locate in urban settings. In such locations they can best avail themselves of needed services and utilities, not to mention labor pools. Urban settings are favored as well because of transportation and communications needs, not to mention other infrastructure requirements. In small economies it does not take huge infusions of production facilities to make significant alterations in urban landscapes. Significant alterations may also occur in public service needs. Many such concerns have been discussed earlier in the current volume.

Certainly, any shift in the direction of the economy toward manufacturing in an urban setting may provide a greater impetus to population movements. Whether this is good or bad depends upon whether or not jobs are actually available in manufacturing, and if not, what other survival options are available in an urban setting. In very small economies such population movements may be quite small in both absolute and relative terms and thus may not generate crises on the scale alluded to elsewhere in this volume. Nonetheless, surplus labor in urban settings is a rather undesirable reality, where it occurs. Very small nations may not supply the informal survival options which are available in large Third World metropolitan areas.

In the urban complexes of small nations employment opportunities constitute an ongoing problem. If the types of service employment referred to earlier in this chapter, together with whatever parallel opportunities exist in manufacturing, do not provide an adequate employment base, development will be impeded. In some small nations a way around this potential impasse has been found in the further extension of service activities.

In advanced economies some services have been described as facilitating agents with respect to the successful pursuit of other types of economic activity (McKee 1988 and 1991a). "Within manufacturing processes inputs from various service cadres may be unrecognizable, but the processes in question might not have been feasible without the contributions of business and engineering consultants and other service subcontractors" (McKee and Tisdell, 1990, 28). Business-related services are identified as facilitators in advanced economies and in the international economy as well.

That being the case, it seems reasonable that certain types of services may emerge as facilitators in the domestic economies of small nations. Most obvious among those would be legal services, accounting, and other service subcategories directly related to business. Financial and insurance services would also fit the facilitator description. Certainly, services such as those mentioned here serve to strengthen economies in which they operate. It should also be mentioned that they are normally housed in an urban environment and by their existence they tend to reinforce and encourage the urban emphasis in the economies in question.

In the world economy various facilitative services have been expanding in step with the needs of multinational firms. It has been suggested that improvements in transportation and communications "have dramatically reduced the cost and time required to acquire services from distant suppliers, and this has expanded the geographic area within which service inputs are bought and sold" (Feketekuty, 1988, 10). Feketekuty goes even further to suggest "International business would not exist without extensive international trade in services" (18). Since small independent nations cannot improve their material positions without trade they are beneficiaries of the improvements in transportation and communications cited here.

DeLisle Worrell (1987), writing about Caribbean microstates, saw the improvement of infrastructure as a major prerequisite for growth (166). "Well-equipped airports with convenient passenger facilities . . . were needed for tourism, . . . deep water ports were essential for major commodity exports, and most countries were in need of reliable electricity and telephone" (166). Clearly, small nations in general require the type of services cited by Worrell in order to ensure efficient contact with the external world. Services providing international linkage functions have much to do with the success of international business and indeed that of the international economy.

As has been suggested elsewhere, "sophisticated arrays of facilitating services may run the gamut from being very helpful to being seriously dysfunctional in terms of their impact upon specific . . . jurisdictions" (McKee and Tisdell, 1990, 30). In small economies with no manufacturing activity to speak of there may be little chance that services can facilitate such activity. In cases where they can, by improving physical and/or economic linkages abroad, their overall impact may still be negative if they encourage the emergence of inopportune activities. Examples abound in cases involving environmentally abusive processes.

In small nations where facilitating services contribute to development by making manufacturing feasible, they, together with their production-based clients, will presumably generate expansionary pressures in urban complexes. Beyond this scenario, various facilitative services operating in the international economy may have impacts in small economies even in the absence of manufacturing activity. Certainly, transportation and communication services make stronger linkages to the world economy. Beyond those, international financial services may also be helpful. Generally speaking, the types of services alluded to here tend to be urban based. Their emergence, while strengthening modern sector activity, will also foster the urban emphasis.

"In some cases the facilitating services have become multinational firms in their own right. When that is the case they may even boast branches in Third World nations" (McKee, 1988, 118). Various small nations have strengthened their economies through the hosting of such activities. By becoming hosts for international services they earn foreign exchange (Demas, 1988 and Abu Amara, 1991) and, of course, provide added employment opportunities in their domestic economies. Demas mentioned various service groups in his discussion, including "engineering design and consulting, large scale construction, petroleum and bauxite technology, tertiary-level education and agronomy" (1988, 144). In addition, he listed offshore university education, health, finance, and information processing. Clearly, specific nations may not be able to avail themselves of the entire menu put forward by Demas. Nonetheless, some small nations have certainly benefitted by hosting cadres of services to be sold to foreigners.

Perhaps the most visible involvements in international services on the part of small Third World jurisdictions have been tourism and international financial services. In many cases the urban centers of small nations have adjusted to include sophisticated arrays of services geared to the global economy. In some cases, although presumably providing needed foreign exchange and employment opportunities, the services in question have few domestic users.

The price to be paid for hosting such services may be a reworking of priorities, whereby the needs of the services supersede other economic considerations. This may result in an infrastructure geared to the services and may even result in structural adjustments in urban places which may render the domestic functions of those places rather difficult to perform. Considerations such as these must be factored in by the planners as they move in the direction of services for export. Controlling the nature and positioning of such services, not to mention the degree of involvement, can reduce negative externalities while at the same time rendering certain presumed benefits attainable.

There is no doubt that small Third World nations which successfully encourage the development of service exports, whether related to the international consumer industry that is tourism or to the sophisticated financial and business needs of the world economy, place additional emphasis upon the role of urban places in their economies. International services will also add to the menu of goods, services, and even skilled personnel to be imported. These imports, aside from impacting trade balances, add further to the urban tilt of the economies in question.

In very small economies such an urban tilt may not be a problem in and of itself. This is so because virtually the entire economy should benefit from opportunities which service-led growth engenders. In such jurisdictions and even in small economies which still have significant segments of population as yet unurbanized, the impact of urban centers upon the national economy will be much greater proportionally than such impacts in larger nations with major metropolitan centers. Because of this it is especially important for small nations to ensure the ongoing physical efficiency of their urban places.

Despite the view held by many economists that manufacturing is the major engine of economic growth and strength, or at least that it is more significant than services, it is the latter group of activities that may afford realistic advancement paths for many small economies. Some such economies have turned to tourism as a vehicle for development. Since tourism is dealt with at some length elsewhere in this volume (Chapter 9), little space will be afforded to it here. Certainly, small economies must balance the potential gains from tourism against very real disadvantages that may accompany it.

In the present context it should be mentioned that tourism can have very significant impacts upon urban settings. It can increase congestion in already crowded areas, thus hurting the efficiency of the urban complex as a setting for expansion. It can force activities geared to local needs to relocate in settings which may be less hospitable. It can greatly expand the demand for imports, including food items. In the case of food it may untrack efforts to supply local needs from domestic sources and thus cause food to become more expensive for local consumers. Planners intending to encourage tourism as an engine of growth should ensure that it keeps a proper balance with the size of the country concerned so as not to overshadow local needs.

Since small economies generally rely upon an urban base for their development, planners should be especially careful to ensure that tourism does not overpower such settings. Cautionary notes to small nations concerning tourism really have to do with proportion rather than a need for total avoidance. Tourism should not be encouraged to the point where it becomes a cost rather than an advantage for the country concerned.

Although services geared to local consumers are hardly at the center of the development process, they do provide jobs in an urban setting. Services geared to facilitating manufacturing processes and their expansion may make a positive contribution in some cases but can hardly ensure the emergence of manufacturing facilities in settings which markets cannot endorse. Services which facilitate operations in the international economy may locate in certain small nations, thus contributing to their expansion. Offshore banking centers are an obvious example of this phenomenon. Although many successful examples exist, no one would suggest that all small nations can attract such activity, let alone benefit from it.

In looking at small Third World nations three characteristics which significantly influence their development potential stand out. First of all, their urban centers are proportionately much more significant in shaping the development of the national economy than is the case in larger nations. Second, modernization appears to require strong linkages to the international economy. Third, service activities, both public and private, play much more central roles in such jurisdictions than may have been the case with other nations. These three considerations are inextricably linked.

Of course, such linkages are most obvious in nations which are virtual city-states. Such nations could hardly survive, let alone prosper, without major involvement with the outside world. Such jurisdictions must rely heavily upon trade to bring them the finished products which they need to support material survival, not to mention improvement in an urbanized economy. In some cases manufacturing for export does play a role, but frequently opportunities of that sort are limited by lack of resources and perhaps even geographical positioning. In such nations it is clearly the service sector which must take up the slack if development is to occur. The most successful small nations have gone beyond public services and market-oriented services for the local economy to services which are sold internationally. The nations which are successful in this last service subgroup appear to be the more fortunate among smaller states with respect to growth potential.

A major reason for their hopeful prospects is that services sold to foreign interests help to pay for needed imports. Small nations cannot be conveniently divided between those of the city-state variety and some residual category. Moving away from obvious city-states one finds a diminishing degree of urban involvement. There are ministates which are relatively small in land area but which still may have a subset of their population residing in nonurbanized circumstances. In such economies all of the circumstances alluded to above with respect to city-states may still apply. As mentioned earlier in this chapter, the nonurban residents of such states still have good access to the urban economy. Beyond such access, however, such economies may have the added advantage of being able to practice a certain amount of import substitution with regard to foodstuffs—a luxury which city-states may not enjoy.

Among small nations with larger land areas the city-state model seems to recede in importance, to be replaced by circumstances whereby major metropolitan areas are both visible and important but appear to function more closely to ways described in neoclassical analysis. Small populations may limit the potential for import substitution involving manufactured goods, but it may be both possible and advisable in agricultural circles. In such nations rural-to-urban migration patterns may resemble those of larger Third World nations. That being the case, discussions concerning urban expansion, the positioning of squatters, and urban environmental management presented earlier in this volume would appear to be pertinent.

No one would compare Kingston, Jamaica, or Guatemala City to Mexico City or Sao Paulo, but lessons learned from megacities should be applied rather than relearned in dealing with emerging metropolitan complexes in small nations. In nations where metropolitan complexes house the leading sectors of their economies the planners must concern themselves with ensuring the physical efficiency of those complexes. Indeed, it would appear that anything short of that will place severe limitations upon the growth prospects of such nations.

Part IV

Some Policy Perspectives

10

A General Overview

Although urban planning is hardly an unfamiliar concept in wealthier nations, it seems clear that to a large extent market forces are driving urban expansion in those nations. Even in cases where planned communities have been developed under governmental auspices, market forces are often relied upon to ensure their continued economic viability. As mentioned earlier (Chapter 1), "this view would have to be modified to accommodate the circumstances of urban centers geared to governmental functions and/or nonprofit services." In the United States, for example, communities have been developed in conjunction with major military installations. However, in that nation the continuing viability of communities of any significant size appears to be dependent upon the exigencies of the marketplace.

Most advanced economies seem to rely upon large metropolitan areas to generate a climate conducive to the successful continuation of wide ranges of profit-seeking activities. The relationship appears to be circular in the sense that the activities in question contribute to the ongoing viability of their metropolitan hosts. By their physical positioning in metropolitan complexes, profit-seeking activities take part in physically configuring those complexes. As suggested in Chapter 1, urban agglomerations retain their functions in national economies in direct proportion to the ongoing success of the activities which they harbor.

It seems clear that metropolitan areas and the activities which they house share certain responsibilities with respect to the continuing success of regional and perhaps national economies. Unfortunately, the mere existence of urban areas or, more specifically, how they are configured, is accompanied by certain structural inflexibilities. These rigidities, together with capital configurations which have lost their viability, may impair the efficiency of local economies. They may represent serious sunk costs, but even in cases where they have been written off, they may represent physical barriers to change. Because they exist and occupy space they become impediments to efficiency. There is little doubt that the closing of industrial facilities becomes a problem for physical planners as well as those concerned with unemployment and shrinking tax receipts.

Just by their ongoing existence, abandoned buildings and industrial sites generate problems related to flexibility. Of course, similar negative externalities are often generated by redundant street patterns and other fixed components of metropolitan infrastructures. If such rigidities are not diffused, the urban agglomerations where they are housed can hardly be expected to retain or improve their operating efficiency. Thus, impediments to growth and change emerge which can impact economic conditions well beyond metropolitan boundaries. In a word, if metropolitan complexes house the strengths of modern economies, those economies will suffer when inflexibilities emerge in the metropolitan mix.

Planning procedures and urban renewal scenarios may not be in accord with actual needs if they are merely aimed at retaining or rejuvenating the traditional structure of major metropolitan areas. Newer urban settings may be better able to offer efficient locations for activities suffering the comparative inefficiencies of older agglomerations. The concentration of various economic activities seems far less essential than it may have been in the past. Thus, flexibility has emerged as a concept which can only be ignored by urban planners at their peril.

In recent years, advanced economies have become service oriented. As might be expected, such a dramatic change in structure is being reflected in urban landscapes. Service activities have become much more significant as causal elements in the growth patterns of large metropolitan complexes in advanced nations. The historical significance of manufacturing to urban growth notwith-standing, the importance which services have attained may have been foreshadowed in the structure of urban places. Public and private services appear to have enjoyed central positions in the physical plans of many cities. At least the cities in question appear to have been constructed around various services. The commercial sector occupied the center of cities giving rise to the term Central Business District (CBD). Thus, despite the historical significance of manufacturing to urban agglomerations, services have had long-standing physical impacts upon urban settings.

The positioning of consumer-related services in metropolitan complexes has been influenced by developments in transportation. The replacement of street railways by motor vehicles has had major impacts on the location of services. Specifically, attention has been drawn away from the center of large urban agglomerations. This migration of the urban marketplace is influencing the expansion patterns of entire urban areas. It may also be responsible in part for various structural difficulties which have emerged in the modern city. Ironically, developments in transportation which appear to have made more flexible metropolitan formats attainable are them-selves generating new inflexibilities.

Some of those inflexibilities are the result of suburban expan-sion, which may not be in tune with the overall needs of the metropolis. New suburban commercial and office establishments can be found lining the major approach routes to cities. If the streets and arteries in question were not built with business needs in mind, congestion becomes a suburban phenomenon. In the United States, as was mentioned in Chapter 1, large city populations are not increasing as rapidly as is the land area of the metropolitan areas in question. Few major urban areas in that nation are free from inopportune peripheral development which constitutes serious impediments to efficiency. Metropolitan fringe areas have become settings for conflicts with respect to the spatial needs of secondary and tertiary activities, not to mention those of the domestic sector. Such conflicts are further complicated by multiple political juris-dictions which may be poorly coordinated. Such circumstances can render metropolitan expansion inopportune if not chaotic.

Differences in the components of the urban infrastructure between segments of metropolitan complexes influence the direction of expansion trends. There is no doubt that efficiency would be served, in most cases, through metropolitan cooperation with respect to dealing with components of the infrastructure. Cooperation is also needed with respect to land use because, as shown in Chapter 1, cities by their very nature are replete with structural rigidities which cause the area which they occupy to expand.

Urban expansion patterns are also influenced by physical geography. It is hardly surprising when land which is most easily accessible and most amenable to development is used first. Transportation choices influence expansion. Auto routes produce strip development while rapid transit generates concentrations of activity at major stations or interchanges. Suburban expansion requires increases in public services. Despite the political fragmentation common to many metropolitan complexes, service efficiency seems best assured by area-wide cooperation. Such cooperation is especially important because of the fact that inflexibilities are built into expansion patterns. The lack of cooperation can further complicate and enlarge inflexibilities, to the detriment of metropolitan efficiency and growth. Thus, metropolitan integration and flexibility should be high on the priority lists of planners.

Transportation technology is both a hero and a villain in the process of urban expansion. It was certainly the railroad or, more specifically, street railways which made the development of very large cities possible but, as discussed in Chapter 1, it was the automobile which made the United States an urban society. It appears as though the motor vehicle has taken over the task of shaping urban expansion. The planners have been cast in a mold of crisis response with respect to keeping the circulatory systems of metropolitan complexes functioning.

Noyelle and Stanback suggested that no real consensus exists concerning the way in which the urban system in the United States is being restructured (1984, 2). If they were correct in their perception that those concerned with urban areas focused on growth rather than the underlying processes of change, why should anyone be surprised at the problems that major metropolitan areas have developed? Without repeating the details of their analysis, which were outlined in Chapter 1, suffice it to say that they see cities emerging as major service centers where manufacturing employment has become much less important. Certainly, measures of growth may easily miss the subtleties of such an adjustment and are hardly a sound basis for planners to provide needed adjustments in the infrastructure, not to mention urban services.

On the surface the structural adjustments which have been occurring in metropolitan complexes in the United States may seem to be led by consumer services. However, Noyelle and Stanback saw those subcategories as playing relatively minor roles (1984, 16). Instead, they attributed the main thrust of service expansion to producer services, government, and nonprofit services. If they were correct in downplaying the actual importance of consumer service, "it may well be that the physical positioning of consumer services may have undue impacts upon metropolitan structure" (see Chapter 1). It seems clear that metropolitan complexes must provide the environment to facilitate production-oriented services aimed at manufacturing processes which may be located elsewhere. Whether such a prescription is represented to a suitable extent in planning processes remains to be seen.

There are dangers in applying perceptions generated in advanced nations to problems in Third World jurisdictions. Despite such difficulties, some cautious comparisons may be useful in reaching an understanding of the role of metropolitan complexes in emerging nations. For example, as indicated in Chapter 2, "If flexibility is a matter of some significance within metropolitan configurations housed in advanced economies, it would appear to be even more important in the major metropolitan areas of the Third World." Urban centers in emerging nations can ill afford the inefficiencies that have accompanied economic change in the metropolitan centers of advanced nations.

In Third World nations, leading modern sector activities tend to position themselves in major metropolitan complexes, thus giving such agglomerations significant impacts on the national economies that house them. As leading sectors grow and change, overall developmental needs change with them. If metropolitan complexes are unable to provide for such needs, development may not proceed. Thus, flexibility must be given high priority by development planners. Unfortunately, flexibility may be an illusive goal within metropolitan settings.

Urban complexes in Third World economies can have major impacts upon national infrastructures. Their positioning appears to be especially pressing in smaller nations. In some cases that positioning can actually constrain development as it has in Central America (see Chapter 2). The manner in which urban complexes develop can have lasting impacts upon national economies. Indeed, many small nations may become little more than city-states. Throughout the Third World development planners who choose to ignore the impacts of major metropolitan complexes do so at their peril, since the national infrastructure will be slanted in the direction of an urbanized economy. There is little doubt that the positioning of cities will impact the direction of development in Third World settings.

In some cases development planners at the national level have recognized the importance of major urban complexes. Such practitioners on occasion have attempted to influence the physical direction of expansion through developing new urban complexes or through attempting to influence the expansion patterns of existing cities. In emerging nations various attempts at altering the direction or momentum of development through city building have occurred. Such projects have met with mixed results. If existing population groupings seem to be positioned by economic considerations or if the leading sectors of the national economy are located in urban complexes, it may not be advisable to alter such realities. Efforts to change the nature or momentum of development through building new cities or moving activities may be problems in themselves.

As mentioned earlier, the bulk of modern sector activities in Third World economies is housed in urban areas which are already in place. Of course, there are exceptions to this in the case of activities related to the primary sector and the location-specific requirements of the tourist industry. By and large economic expansion is heavily concentrated in urban areas. The task for the planners is not the diffusion of such expansion, which may be impractical, but rather its facilitation. Of course, those concerned with growth and development may have to face problems related to the complexities of urban locations, "not the least of which may be the seemingly inopportune positioning of urban complexes as judged by economic needs" (see Chapter 2). Real-world experience falls short of supporting the construction of new cities as a work-able solution. A more sensible and less costly approach which planners should consider is the promotion of the ongoing viability of existing urban areas.

Unfortunately, continuing viability may be a rather elusive goal in major Third World urban areas. Since urban settings are inextricably linked to economic growth, mere success in that vein turns them into impacted areas. Problems which are size related are all but inevitable. Size itself can become an issue where it stifles economic activity or prevents change. Ironically, problems of that nature are not confined to the huge metropolitan complexes that capture the attention of the media. They can be found in relatively small urban areas where infrastructure components have not kept up with needs or where they cannot be altered to meet changing conditions. Thus, the major problem may not be size alone but rather flexibility.

Concerns about the role of urbanization in growth processes are hardly new to economists. If cities seem to be focal points for growth and change it should not be surprising if those concerned with economic expansion in emerging nations are displaying on-going interests in them. Those interests have been fueled by a system of thought known as pole theory, which has emerged during the second half of this century. In addressing the ways in which leading economic activities determine the direction of growth, it is hardly surprising that some proponents of pole theory have come to focus on urban complexes. Growth poles are the leading industrial sectors of an economy. If they are generally to be found in urban settings, it is probably safe to suggest that such locations are heavily involved in the processes of growth and change.

As change occurs leading sectors are replaced, necessitating adjustments in the urban areas that host the activities in question. If such urban areas fail to adjust, growth processes will be impacted adversely. Once again flexibility emerges as an essential planning objective. As discussed in Chapter 2, even though cities seem to provide the climate for various economic activities, there is no assurance that specific urban areas will remain prosperous simply because they exist. Their prosperity will depend upon their ability to adapt to the needs of a continuously changing selection of economic units.

Among the economic activities emerging in Third World metropolitan areas are production facilities of multinational firms. Such firms are locating in Third World settings with an eye to supplying their international clients. They choose their locations in keeping with their needs for international linkages, not to mention a suitable labor pool and local business environment. Urban areas that are chosen as locations for such activities can make major contributions to domestic expansion.

A downside risk exists in the sense that the production facilities that are hosted are hardly immune to crises and/or changes in the international economy. Adverse overspills from international circumstances can interfere with the domestic development objectives of host nations. In cases where permanent negative adjustments occur, urban areas can be left with redundant infrastructure components, not to mention noticeable gaps or declines in modern sector activity. Once again flexibility seems to be a serious issue. Development which is highlighted by the success of foreign manufacturing facilities can be threatened by those operations if they fail.

As pointed out in Chapter 2, change under the best of conditions can be painful. Third World metropolitan areas, because they host many of the activities of the modern sectors of their national economies, can expect to be faced with continuous change. Change (growth?) can be expected to favor some activities over others. In urban environments the growth or decline of specific firms or industries causes serious flexibility concerns. A failure to deal with those concerns may destroy the climate for economic expansion.

In some metropolitan complexes, expanding populations add to flexibility problems and yet flexibility is not simply a function of population absorption. Development depends upon the emergence of a viable and expanding modern sector which can underwrite an expansionist climate. The activities which compose the modern sector must be capable of ongoing, positive domestic impacts. Those with developmental responsibilities must ensure that the urban areas under their jurisdiction have infrastructures and service complements adequate for the needs of an ever-changing cohort of industrial units.

Activities need not be of the leading sector variety to generate ongoing positive impacts. Pursuits which provide jobs and outlets for unemployed resources can certainly contribute to economic improvement as characterized by the growth of modern sector activity. The positive impacts from such activities will undoubtedly put pressure on the urban areas housing them. Because of relatively limited domestic markets as a result of dualism, export-oriented activities would seem to hold more immediate potential for generating growth than would those aimed at local customers. Accessing foreign markets generates income for consumers and thus encourages the expansion of domestic markets. If the production-oriented activities are carried out in urban settings, those areas must be capable of efficient physical expansion and adjustment. Thus, urban areas should be among the concerns of those responsible for developmental initiatives at the national level. "The search for urban efficiency and flexibility in Third World settings is very much a macroeconomic issue" (see Chapter 2).

It is becoming clear that modern sector activities of the type which can be relied upon as stimuli for growth and change in Third World economies tend to locate in urban settings. The truth of this is no guarantee that lasting improvements will come about. At the national level the successful functioning of an economy that is urban based is dependent upon changes in agriculture which free labor to follow new urban opportunities. Beyond greater efficiency, the agricultural components of the economy must address the issue of supplying the food needs of the domestic population. Failure in this regard will make the urban focus of the economy a costly one reliant upon food imports. Since market forces may not address this problem effectively, it may need to be considered by planning authorities at the national level. Successful development seems to be prefaced upon import substitution in agriculture and a reduced reliance upon primary exports.

Of course, successful adjustments in agriculture will hardly guarantee that economic growth will follow. Such adjustments make urban-based expansion more feasible, but it must be remembered, "Urbanization is a necessary but by no means a sufficient condition for economic development" (McKee and Leahy, 1974). Urban settings can bring with them various rigidities that are capable of impeding development. Although advanced economies appear to be urban based, those very urban environments can block adjustments in the mix of activities because of the fact that they were customized to meet earlier needs.

Many Third World jurisdictions have been experiencing major shifts in population toward major metropolitan areas. Unfortunately, a direct correlation between a population influx and the growth of successful modern sector activities in urban complexes cannot be assumed. Indeed, even the assumptions that successful pursuits will remain so and that the urban areas hosting them will continue to grow and prosper may be unwarranted. It would seem advisable for planning initiatives to emphasize flexibility if metropolitan complexes are to remain successful as settings for sustained growth.

There is little question that the concentration of economic activity in metropolitan areas will reinforce spatial imbalances which can be expected in market-oriented economies (see McKee, 1991a). Imbalances are unavoidable in profit-driven economies. Public policy initiatives aimed at them directly may be ill-advised unless the imbalances in question are impeding development and thus retarding the ability of the economy to improve the material welfare of the population. "One way in which the imbalances in question may be impeding material progress is through an implicit support of dualism" (Chapter 3). If a modern economy is superimposed upon a more traditional one, the former may be urban based. In that setting it may draw resources from rural areas. This causes urban areas in question to expand. Whether or not they become stronger requires an analysis of how incoming populations fare and how they impact urban settings.

Expanding urban populations place ever-increasing demands on social overhead capital and ever-increasing pressures on urban infrastructures. Such pressures and demands, when left unmet, will contribute to urban inflexibilities which in turn may damage the efficiency of the economy. Third World economies require serious attention to urban planning if they intend to rely upon metropolitan complexes as settings for economic development led by modern sector activities. Maintaining a climate conducive to expansion requires that attention be paid to meeting both present and anticipated future needs of modern sector activities. In other words, planners must facilitate urban settings which change with the needs of their components.

As mentioned earlier, rural-to-urban migration is increasing in Third World economies and new arrivals in metropolitan complexes have few skills to offer in urban labor markets. Labor absorption is hardly the automatic process that certain neoclassical thinkers have presumed it to be. Beyond that, few city governments are able to deal with such rapid growth (Tisdell, 1990, 117). Nonetheless, the processes of development and urbanization appear to be linked inextricably. Dualism in labor markets may impede development. Neoclassical analyses suggest that as surplus labor enters urban labor markets it must be absorbed if progress is to be sustained. Continuing in-migration tends to depress wages in the most menial urban occupations, but there may be little ability for modern sector activities to absorb the continuing flow at any price.

Those who are not gaining modern sector employment are finding other means of survival. In some cases this means an existence based upon barter or some form of self-employment. This seems to support the existence of an ongoing, perhaps even permanent type of urban dualism. Where it exists, efficient expansion of metropolitan areas will face serious difficulties. As suggested by Roberts, urban settings cause the consumption of the poor to become dependent upon the market (1978, 112). In other words, their budgets may come to include ever-larger expenditures on goods and services originating in the modern sector. Presumably, such a dependence would not be accompanied by increasing job opportunities for the poor. Of course, such a circumstance should be of major concern to the planners, since an increasing population (the poor) seems to have little chance of becoming a part of a group process which relies upon modern sector activity that excludes that rising population.

Despite the negative tone of the last paragraph the urban setting, granting its problems, may present a better potential for survival than rural alternatives. Even in the face of real drawbacks, the experience and even modest financial gains which nonparticipants in modern sector activities may acquire in urban settings may improve their future prospects, while permitting their immediate survival. This, of course, can be expected to encourage a continuing flow of in-migrants, which no doubt complicates the tasks of the planners.

For impacted urban centers the problems related to the continuing population influx are more immediate than those surrounding the issue of labor absorption. The burgeoning population places additional demands upon the local economy for social overhead capital. Such demands may well alter government priorities in ways that impede the creation of an infrastructure suited to the needs of economic expansion. In other words, rising populations may introduce inflexibilities which may well impede economic expansion. Indeed, rising populations can actually set the dimensions and physical characteristics of metropolitan complexes and in doing so may damage the efficiency of the complexes in question. Negative externalities may well be felt beyond urban boundaries. Thus, those responsible for ensuring the growth potential of national economies should be concerned.

In Third World settings where infrastructures are being extended beyond urban areas, employment opportunities in newly reached areas may succumb to the improved accessibility of larger urban areas. Even in rural areas a better level of integration with urban complexes may destroy old livelihoods. The sometimes hackneyed accusations of urban bias or suggestions involving reducing the flow of rural-to-urban migration may be out of step with the realities of the forces at work. Instead, planning time may be better spent in ensuring that metropolitan complexes retain the flexibility needed to sustain growth and change. Too often planning procedures are cast in a crisis-response format. Facilitation of growth and change must be written into planning procedures at both local and national levels if metropolitan areas are to be relied upon as settings for development in Third World nations.

11

Structural and Environmental Imperatives

The major, ongoing population increases which Third World metropolitan areas are experiencing are creating problems that, on occasion, extend beyond the physical bounds of impacted urban complexes to interfere with the development potential of national economies. This is so because many of the leading sectors of Third World economies are housed in metropolitan complexes. At any point in time the ability of those modern sector activities to absorb additional labor may be quite limited. Many of the new arrivals in Third World cities are unskilled and have few illusions concerning their marketability. Objectives other than employment opportunities in the modern sector are generating population movements. Thus, cities are increasing in population much more rapidly than their capacity to absorb labor, a reality which impacts their development, if not that of national economies.

As surplus labor emerges in urban settings, slums proliferate. As in-migration continues, increasing demands are placed upon local economies for social overhead capital. In some cases these demands may cause adjustments in the priorities of the planners, which in turn can drain public funds, thus retarding the creation of an infrastructure suitable for economic expansion. Such drains on public funds can go beyond local sources to access federal pools, thus necessitating adjustments in priorities at the national level.

The potential for national development can also be affected if increasing urban populations impede the efficiency of modern sector activities. In urban complexes the mere positioning of the poor can impede efficiency. In many Third World settings slums are a problem of the urban periphery which, by their mere existence, can impose obstacles to the growth of the urban economy. In such urban complexes, the growth of modern sector activities may intensify within the area encircled by slums, thus encouraging difficulties associated with congestion. As an alternative, modern sector development may leapfrog over the slums and thus generate difficulties with respect to the integration of the urban economy. If the local authorities extend roads and public services through squatter settlements they give those areas a degree of permanence. If the settlements in question interfere with the expansion of the urban infrastructure they will impede development. Simply because slums occupy space, they force an increasing cost framework upon expansion projects with respect to the infrastructure (see Chapter 4).

When existing settlements exhaust their capacity to absorb more population, new settlements form elsewhere in a happenstance fashion. "If Third World metropolitan areas grow in this fashion, squatter settlements are actually determining both growth patterns and the eventual configuration of the urban complex" (see Chapter 4). The continuing influx of migrants causes problems with respect to the physical structure of cities. This causes serious concerns for those involved in planning processes. Existing squatter settlements are an accomplished fact. Their removal is often impractical and their continued presence contributes to congestion and structural inefficiencies. Surplus labor and surplus population in general place increasing demands upon urban services. Providing such services may result in an inopportune rearrangement of government priorities which may well impede overall efforts at developmental planning.

Although serious costs seem apparent, in some ways squatter settlements may play positive roles in urban areas. Their inhabitants may enjoy services which would have been much less available in rural settings. Through such services residents may increase their productivity potential, thus improving their chances for employment in the modern sector. Some residents of squatter settlements do enter modern sector pursuits over time, but many do not. Thus, the squatter settlements may become semipermanent living spaces for those who inhabit them.

The general elimination of squatter settlements from the urban complexes of the Third World is not an attainable goal. They will remain unless poverty is eliminated. Realism suggests that squatter settlements should hold a regular place in the discussions of planners and policymakers. More specifically, those officials should make an effort to ensure that settlements do not impede the orderly and efficient development of metropolitan areas. Planning should also embrace concerns for the basic safety and human dignity of the residents of squatter settlements. In line with the suggestions enumerated here, it seems ill-advised to provide for gradual upgrading of settlements, with the intention of removing them from the squatter category. Such a goal, if brought to fruition, might well ensure that improving settlements would be replaced by others as bad or worse, which would cause additional uncertainties for the planners.

Since there is a continuing influx of population destined for squatter settlements in many Third World urban areas, the expansion of areas given over to squatters can only be retarded by encouraging earlier residents to move on if and when their material status improves. Unfortunately, migrants who enter squatter settlements may not anticipate moving again. In theory at least, squatter settlements would become unnecessary if poverty were eliminated. However, not all residents of squatter settlements are poor. Many stay in such settings well beyond the time that necessity requires. Their presence limits the ability of existing settlements to absorb new migrants, which of course causes the emergence of more or larger settlements. "Unnecessary slums are unquestionably a drain on public funds and beyond that may very well interfere with the efficient expansion of urban complexes" (Chapter 4).

In Third World economies urban slums are often arranged in a haphazard fashion. Squatter settlements are perhaps the most unpredictable, since they can vary in size from small, village-like neighborhoods to huge complexes with hundreds of thousands of inhabitants. Their unpredictability is further enhanced by the fact that they can appear almost anywhere. It is this unpredictability that should concern the planners.

Slums and/or squatter settlements cannot be permitted to interfere with efficient urban expansion. Failure in this regard may retard general developmental objectives and with them the potential for improving the material status of large segments of the population. Within this general framework the idea of supporting the improvement of slum property requires careful assessment. If slums are unavoidable and perhaps even needed, then their position within the metropolitan complex should be planned. A fringe benefit from such planning will be a reduction in their negative impact upon the city.

If slums are positioned by planning it seems logical to opt for at least a minimum level of social overhead capital and public services for them. Of course, such inputs should be provided in consort with the goal of deciding where the slums should be and keeping them there. The planned positioning of slums seems incompatible with the objective of upgrading squatter settlements to the point where they are eliminated. Livable slums should be preserved as such with the proviso that surplus slums should be removed on a worst-first basis. Unsafe settlements must share top billing on any removal list with those which are interfering with the efficient operation of the metropolitan economy.

Certainly, the slum as a planning concept is a significant idea. The creation of conditions supportive of human dignity and safety in necessary slums should be given high priority by the planners. The sidestepping of issues related to squatters, their needs, and the impacts which they are making in urban areas may result in insurmountable planning problems in the future.

The transition of labor from rural to urban settings may not be the orderly process that many economists have envisioned. Nonetheless, it seems clear that market forces are driving the migrations. People move in hopes of ensuring survival and perhaps material improvement. Ways to stem the migratory flow are far from evident. As a consequence, development specialists and planners find themselves in a crisis-response mode. They must respond if they are to ensure that impacted urban areas can provide a setting for economic expansion, not to mention improving human circumstances.

As pointed out in Chapter 4, migrants may be reasonably realistic with respect to what they hope to accomplish in an urban setting. Their objective may not be to find employment in the modern sector. Instead they may feel that the informal activities available to them in the city will sustain them. Certainly, the residents of squatter settlements appear to have an implicit understanding of their economic self-interests. Because informal sector activities are providing them with both subsistence and opportunities for economic improvement over time, the signal appears to be positive and migration will continue and perhaps increase in scope. Of course, an increasing squatter population broadens the market for the offerings of the informal sector.

The need to provide space for squatters in urban complexes seems self-evident. Failure to do so will not stop the migratory flow. As it continues, settlements develop that may interfere with the efficient operation and expansion of urban complexes. Planning can certainly reduce that problem as well as difficulties associated with the emergence of unsafe settlements. Sensible planning procedures should allow for a continuing influx of people.

"Massive relocation projects involving squatter communities may be difficult if not impossible" (Chapter 4). The elimination of unacceptable squatter settlements may be a long and tedious task. Settlements which interfere with economic efficiency are probably the easiest to eliminate. For instance, if the land which they occupy could be better used for modern sector activities, the market may make it possible to compensate residents for relocating. The compensation may be from either public or business sources and may include a better array and/or quality of urban services in new locations. By selecting locations for squatters, development planners may be able to make certain services available at reasonable costs. In doing that the planners make the areas chosen more attractive for potential residents.

In cases where poorly located squatter settlements encumber the efficient integration of the metropolis rather than the use of marketable land, the problems may be more intractable. Beyond the inefficiencies which are apparent, existing settlements may not lend themselves to elimination through market-supported compensation. Thus, removal may be difficult and the inefficiencies will continue. As mentioned earlier, expansion patterns will have to move beyond the settlements in an increasing cost framework. If this involves the extension of urban services through squatter settlements it may make those areas more attractive to their residents and as a consequence more difficult to move. The removal of such settlements by force is generally not recommended. The same is not true for settlements that are dangerous. If it is logical to prevent the emergence of settlements in flood plains or other hazardous areas, it is equally logical to plan their removal where they exist. Since dangerous settings are of little economic importance they may lend themselves to settlement. When such areas are settled the squatters will have to be removed at public expense, since private interests will have little incentive to provide compensation. Removal of dangerous settlements is a long-range goal, but prevention must receive ongoing attention.

When land has been set aside for settlements and the plans for eliminating undesirable communities are in place, it remains to consider the needs of settlements judged as necessary. In needed settlements certain urban services should be provided. Residents who improve their material status should be encouraged to move on, thus keeping the settlements available to those without better options. Where possible, settlements should be planned or encouraged in areas where their residents will have access to work opportunities. There is little point in housing people where they will be isolated from urban job markets. In the short run such people will probably seek sustenance from the informal sector, but within a broader time frame access to urban labor markets may become important.

It seems clear that the urban poor and their housing arrangements deserve the concern of the most conservative planners. On pragmatic grounds, it hardly pays to ignore such matters since to do so will only serve to make developmental planning more difficult over time. Indeed, metropolitan areas where these issues are ignored may lose their viability as settings for economic growth.

A major goal of metropolitan planning must be assuring the ability for urban complexes to grow and change while remaining efficient throughout the process. As cities expand they find themselves constrained by narrow streets and difficult traffic patterns. Population increases tax supplies of water and energy. Growth may also threaten the ability to supply other essential services if revenue sources are unable to keep pace. As urban populations continue their upward spiral it is inevitable that the physical dimensions of impacted agglomerations expand as well. Such expansion may even surpass what is needed to accommodate population increases. Even in cases where commercial and industrial expansion lag behind that of population, such pursuits tend to increase the physical size of urban complexes. Such adjustments can hardly be ignored by the planners.

As urban complexes expand their boundaries more attention must be given to the nature and direction of such expansion. Specifically, attention must be directed toward the impact of the expansion of urban peripheries on the cohesion and operating efficiency of metropolitan complexes. One set of impacts deserving of attention involves the issues related to the absorption of existing urban agglomerations by expanding metropolitan complexes. Just as slums can dictate urban growth patterns, other problems relating to the urban periphery can do so as well. Clearly, the absorption of urban agglomerations with functions predating their encounter with metropolitan expansion is one such issue.

In the developed world the expansion of large metropolitan areas is often characterized by the absorption of smaller cities or towns which lose their spatial integrity. Related issues emerge when existing centers are joined by transportation networks or the disappearance of open lands. Such mergers may result in multinucleated metropolitan areas with no obvious center of gravity or cohesiveness.

There is little doubt that the absorption of urban places with their own identities independent of larger centers is adding a new dimension to the overall concerns of uncontrolled expansion in Third World jurisdictions. The problems of human adjustment caused by such changes can be just as traumatic as those facing migrants from rural areas. In some cases smaller urban centers are actually engulfed by metropolitan expansion. In other circumstances highway expansion makes the land in the vicinity of small towns attractive for development. Local labor markets can suffer eclipse and those who relied upon them may find their livelihoods threatened. Beyond the loss of income, small-town residents may also experience declines in local services. Younger, more ambitious small-town residents may leave those areas in search of broader opportunities in metropolitan labor markets.

Despite obvious difficulties smaller urban areas may be able to maintain their physical integrity within metropolitan complexes. If the transportation improvements which come with metropolitan expansion merely provide access to land in the vicinity of smaller urban areas, their physical integrity may not be threatened. More disruptive results may occur if smaller centers are actually on expanding highways. Land use patterns may change if property values increase to the point where owners can no longer retain their property in its traditional role. The environmental integrity of smaller communities may change dramatically.

As change occurs jobs may disappear, traditional commercial relationships may weaken and the residents of smaller communities may find less service and support available. The future well-being of residents will depend upon their ability to enter the new metropolitan mix. It seems likely that the expanding metropolis may destroy the social and economic integrity of smaller communities. Even though such areas may survive in a physical sense the life-styles of their residents may be altered dramatically.

Granting that the impacts of metropolitan absorption may be chaotic in smaller communities, they will also be felt by the metropolitan complexes in general. Small town absorption increases both the population and the land area that metropolitan areas encompass. Small urban enclaves or some which may not be small can cause major discontinuities in metropolitan mosaics. They tend to interfere with the orderly expansion of metropolitan space and complicate the process of service expansion. Viewed from a metropolitan vantage point the continued existence of small, peripheral communities may well be at odds with functional land use patterns and may actually be interfering with the efficiency of the metropolitan economy.

It seems impractical to recommend the demolition or removal of urban communities in the path of metropolitan expansion. However, potential negative impacts from their merger with the metropolis may be capable of being reduced by judicious preplanning. By planning the location of transportation and service facilities it may be possible to keep metropolitan expansion away from such communities. Where physical mergers appear to be unavoidable, planners must give priority to the efficient provision of services throughout the entire metropolitan complex in keeping with the need for efficiency and cohesiveness.

When emergent metropolitan areas, created by the coming to-gether of existing communities become destinations for surplus labor, their integrity may be impaired. New arrivals will want to settle in sites which provide reasonable survival options. For ex-ample, they will want to locate near existing job opportunities in modern sector pursuits. In multinucleated metropolitan areas service opportunities may be more plentiful and accessible than in comparable centers with a conventional central business district. Thus, entry-level opportunities in the modern sector may be a stronger population magnet in multinucleated metropolitan areas. The multinucleated metropolitan complex as it develops may prove to be an especially attractive destination for migrants, since open land within the area gives squatters convenient access. Such complexes may actually become impacted by in-migrants because of potential opportunities in both services and the informal sector.

As the multinucleated complex comes together, economic inte-gration and the provision of urban services can become serious problems. Planners should become involved in ensuring the over-all efficiency of the metropolis. Since getting a planning organiza-tion together, which represents the constituent parts of the metropolitan complex may be difficult, a higher authority may be needed. Any planning authority should place the development of an infrastructure which facilitates the integration of the emerging metropolis high on its priority list. In addition, planners should opt to ensure an efficient and fair distribution of urban services.

Once again it must be emphasized that planners should control both the positioning and servicing of squatter settlements. They should show special concern for the positioning of new arrivals. In the case of multinucleated urban areas, they may have more flexi-bility. For instance, they may be able to encourage the formation of settlements in safe settings. They may also be able to ensure that new arrivals are well positioned with respect to access to work and also regarding the supply of basic services. Fast action is indicated if an efficient metropolitan mix is to be assured.

Hindsight seems to suggest that metropolitan planning in emerging nations should avoid the crisis-response mode when possible. This implies a more activist planning philosophy which seeks to prevent crises before they emerge. If multinucleated complexes are permitted to emerge happenstance or if metropolitan areas are permitted to expand at random, crisis-response measures will still be required. Unfortunately, crisis diffusion is hardly a foundation for economic efficiency.

Crises can emerge from environmental concerns as well as from the issues discussed above. A reduction in the coping ability of the natural environment vis-à-vis urbanization can interfere with both growth and development. Cities may be necessary in any functional economy, but cities with poorly managed environments can cause both economic and physical problems which may have impacts well beyond urban boundaries. With respect to environmental issues international interdependence seems irrefutable.

In the Third World, large metropolitan complexes have emerged which are creating environmental difficulties on a massive scale. In some instances environmental difficulties associated with production are being ignored by the planners on the grounds that manufacturing processes are creating jobs. The level of environmental difficulties may increase more rapidly than population in Third World settings. In some cases climate and topography may be factors to the extent that they impact the ability of nature to defuse environmental problems. Clearly, various environmental concerns may reinforce each other and thus become more difficult to deal with in metropolitan complexes. As Tisdell has suggested, urbanization and industrialization combine to generate concentrations of waste, and the failure to intervene can cause health problems and even problems with production (1990). Katzman saw environmental pressures as proportional to the rate of growth as opposed to mere population size (1977). As suggested in Chapter 6, "In taking that position he was . . . giving implicit recognition to the inflexibilities of infrastructure components faced with population growth."

Certainly, rigidities in the components of urban infrastructures concerned with environmental matters can interfere with growth and change. As previously pointed out (Chapter 6), Katzman saw difficulties which were independent of city size and also independent of the level of urbanization in the nation concerned (1977, 175). It seems clear that planners who view urban areas as the setting for modern sector activities and thus growth and development can hardly ignore environmental matters.

The continuing influx of population which metropolitan complexes in emerging nations are experiencing presents a unique set of environmental difficulties. Of course, the expansion of industry in urban settings is presenting difficulties as well. Contrary to what might be expected, new arrivals in urban squatter settlements may not create automatic overloads with respect to the provision of public services. Squatters often enjoy few of the urban services which are often taken for granted in more affluent settings. Nonetheless, the magnitude of squatter components in metropolitan areas demands that environmental difficulties generated in the settlements be dealt with. It matters little that planners have the power to withhold any or all public services from squatter settlements. In practice it may make little sense to deny access to services impacting the environment.

Some such services, if withheld, may allow serious negative impacts to develop. Among those services would be the disposal of sewerage and other forms of waste. In many squatter communities options are limited with respect to the disposal of sewerage. Improperly dealt with sewerage may contaminate water supplies, encourage insect populations, and perhaps foster disease. Obviously, the negative externalities associated with such matters may be felt well beyond the confines of squatter settlements. Perhaps the removal of sewerage is an example of a public service that the planners may be well advised to provide. Sewerage removal will generate the greatest positive impact upon metropolitan areas only if it is treated before its ultimate release.

In squatter settlements a related issue revolves around the handling of garbage and cast-off materials. Ironically, in some cases the recovery of materials by the poor may reduce the pressure on metropolitan dump sites. Nonetheless, due to the extent of squatter settlements in the metropolitan complexes of emerging nations, the garbage which they generate should be of major concern. Such densely settled areas generate considerable cast-off material. Its disposal by metropolitan authorities deserves careful consideration in order to minimize negative externalities which may well interfere with growth and development. Certain services must be provided in squatter communities in the interests of economic efficiency. Beyond those mentioned, safe water should also be considered. By providing clean water the quality of life and the environment can be improved appreciably, to the benefit of the whole urban complex.

Refusal or inability to deal with issues such as those referred to above may impede necessary growth and change in urban complexes. In some cases this can be detrimental to growth at the national level. As suggested in chapter 6, "All environmental issues involving squatter settlements must be weighed and prioritized in keeping with the needs and objectives of general development."

In many cases production facilities that are fouling the environment are components of multinational firms. In some cases such facilities were established due to permissive attitudes on the part of public authorities toward activities which threaten the environment. Certainly planners should establish some form of understanding with firms wishing to establish plants. Any such understanding should include concerns for the environment. In agreeing to host manufacturing plants those concerned may be making trade-offs between a certain level of environmental damage and the perceived benefits with respect to growth which the facilities in question may generate. Those engaged in development planning should weigh the advantages and disadvantages of every proposal in advance of accepting polluting facilities. The decisions which are made should probably reflect domestic needs rather than an international agenda.

In some cases expanded employment opportunities may have to be weighed against short-run, negative exernalities and environmental damage which may even be permanent. Obviously, planners who elect to accept dirty manufacturing processes are doing so pragmatically. A part of their decision should include the actual location of the plants. In some cases permitting the plants to locate in major metropolitan areas may not be cost-effective. Less-crowded areas may be more advantageous. Unfortunately, the feasibility of nonmetropolitan locations may be constrained by the infrastructure. Market forces, if left to their own devices, may tend to concentrate activities in urban settings. Environmental difficulties in Third World metropolitan areas afford no easy solutions. Like other issues alluded to in this chapter, they require the careful attention of the planners. Environmental difficulties which may be capable of impeding growth and change should receive special attention.

12

Some Final Reflections

Despite the fact that many Third World nations are still export-ing primary products, their roles in the global economy have expanded well beyond the supplying of such commodities. More global involvements have come with the adoption of goals related to growth and development. Of course, foreign linkages have impacted the structure of the economies in question and in some cases the urban sectors of those economies. Such impacts can hardly be ignored by those concerned with overall developmental objectives.

During the colonial era advanced nations showed little interest in forming general developmental objectives for territories from which they obtained staple commodities. Where development did occur it was geared to getting out the staples and not toward any general objectives of concern to the jurisdictions in question. As shown in Chapter 7, "Whether Third World nations tracing their economic roots to staple exports can use those roots as the founda-tion for sustained economic advances is hardly self-evident."

There is little doubt that staples have impacted the direction of development in certain parts of the world, but they should be viewed with caution as means for generating economic expansion today. In this century the terms of trade have turned against staple commodities. Nations that relied upon such exports may not have prepared foundations for growth or development. Too much emphasis may have been placed upon infrastructures geared mainly to getting out the staples, rather than to general development. Dating from colonial times this has meant an emphasis upon staple-oriented port facilities and transportation linkages. The emphasis upon ports and colonial administration encouraged population expansion in certain urban areas and, of course, impacted the physical structure of those areas. Such developments caused the commitment of public funds to the expansion of urban services and investments in social overhead capital which lent a degree of permanence to how and where urban areas had been configured. In some cases involving extractive activities, the potential for sunk costs has been especially serious. Rigidities resulting from primary production for export may easily do serious damage to efficient expansion at the national level.

Difficulties caused by urban areas configured to accommodate the export of staples are not the only way in which primary export activities are impacting urban development. In nations where staple exports continue to be emphasized in spite of negative terms of trade, pressures exist to increase their quantity to counterbalance the higher costs of imports. If the quantity increases are brought about by mechanization, workers are displaced from the primary sector. Such displacements fuel rural-to-urban migration, thus contributing to the types of urban difficulties discussed at length in the current volume.

Dualism can cause difficulties associated with urbanization and economic integration in Third World settings. Where dualism exists infrastructures are slanted toward the modern economy. Since modern sector activities tend to gravitate toward urban areas, those locations have their gravitational pull magnified by improving infrastructures. Thus, a strong urban emphasis in the economy becomes a fait accompli. Government decisions in support of modern sector activities reinforce urban expansion and thus increase the responsibilities of those concerned with the urban planning issues referred to in this volume.

As manufacturing activities develop in emerging nations the role of cities is strengthened. This is so because urban areas hold the most attractive locational choices for production facilities. As such facilities expand, the urban areas that house them are faced with an increasing demand for infrastructure components and urban services. Industrialization places increasing pressure on urban planners not just because of infrastructure and services, but also because the positioning of production units will have a general impact upon the physical structure of urban configurations. As shown in Chapter 7, "the positioning of manufacturing facilities is yet another element, which together with the location of new arrivals to the urban complex . . . . and the absorption of existing urban agglomerations . . . must be considered if expanding urban mosaics are to be assured of continuing economic viability." Even planners at the national level should be concerned with the nature and positioning of production facilities because of the impact which urban agglomerations have upon national development.

Of course, the global basis of decision making is one of the more serious issues related to the hosting of foreign owned production facilities (see Chapter 7). Corporate planners make their decisions in keeping with company-wide objectives which may be influenced by cost cutting and the maintenance of profitability as well as access to local markets. Where location decisions are made in search of local energy services or more permissive environmental regulations, local planners must be alert to ensure that proposed corporate plans are in keeping with local developmental needs and objectives.

This is especially applicable to decisions involving the building of infrastructures. Because production facilities are most likely to be urban based, the infrastructure which is called for may impact the physical structure of cities. Since foreign-owned plants will be designed to accommodate the needs of their firms in world markets and will thrive or fail based upon the exigencies of these markets, the infrastructure which they require may or may not be helpful in terms of general developmental goals and may become redundant or counterproductive should the plants themselves fail. Planners are not gatekeepers who should refuse to support the legitimate needs of corporate players, but in meeting such needs they must maintain a broader perspective which includes the more general needs of their jurisdictions. In short, infrastructure components should not be so selectively designed as to deny assistance to general developmental goals or to be unusable should their major corporate users disappear. These concerns are especially pertinent in urban areas where flexibility is important.

In order to meet general developmental goals planners must take part in corporate locational decisions. It is especially important that they take part in such decisions in metropolitan complexes. As discussed in Chapter 7, there may be serious problems for planners with respect to obtaining information from their corporate counterparts. Such problems are made more difficult if the corporate planners are not resident in the jurisdictions concerned. Lack of cooperation on the part of corporate planners would appear to be a clear signal for those concerned with development in specific Third World jurisdictions. Everything may be negotiable before the arrival of the contemplated production facilities. After their arrival little may be capable of adjustment. "Clearly, the planners should be active if they hope to ensure that urban and even national infrastructures meet domestic as well as export needs" (Chapter 7).

Urban planners should be concerned about the positioning of production facilities owned by multinational firms and geared to export markets. They should also be concerned about the infrastructure that such facilities may require and most particularly with how that infrastructure may facilitate or impede broader developmental objectives. Such concerns are especially important in an urban context where the maintenance of flexibility is a serious issue.

The concerns expressed in the preceding paragraph apply equally to changes which have been occurring due to the unprecedented expansion which the international travel industry has been enjoying in Third World settings. In advanced nations tourism has often been a catalyst in urban and regional development. Such successes have not gone unnoticed in the Third World. Many emerging nations have turned to tourism as a potential contributor to their economic betterment. Once again advanced planning is indicated, especially in cases where major tourist facilities are contemplated for urban locations.

Any Third World nation aspiring to host successful tourist ventures will have to invest in a transportation and communications infrastructure geared to international travel. In most Third World jurisdictions existing components of transportation and communications infrastructures tend to be located so as to serve the needs of urban areas or, more specifically, the needs of businesses in such areas for linkages. Thus, "the advent of tourism reinforces the strength of those infrastructure components and with them the urban emphasis in the host country" (Chapter 8).

The case for encouraging mass tourism in Third World jurisdictions is strong or weak depending upon how the industry may impact domestic employment opportunities and foreign exchange balances. Beyond such concerns is "the potential impact that the industry may have upon the local culture and environment, resource utilization and the general quality of life" (Chapter 8). Most of the concerns listed here have been recognized by economists and others concerned with development.

The impact that tourism may have upon urban environments in the Third World has received much less attention. Because those environments are conducive to mass tourism they may well incur the most serious impacts from it. There is little question that the potential impact of tourism in such settings should be considered by the planners with respect to how it influences general development aims. Specifically, it is important to ascertain the impact of tourism in urban settings on the role of those settings in development. Certainly, it appears as though planners may do well to exercise caution when faced with the potential for an uncontrolled expansion of tourist capacity. In Third World settings diversification should be an important objective.

There is no doubt that Third World jurisdictions electing tourism as a major component of their development efforts increase their exposure to events beyond their control. The emergence of new competitors and changing tourist tastes, not to mention shifts in emphasis on the part of multinational firms within the industry, may alter the fortunes of specific host nations.

The uncertainties of the industry have clear implications for Third World metropolitan areas. In cases where such centers undergo substantial adjustments in order to accommodate tourism it would seem advisable to look beyond tourism as well in order to ensure that declining fortunes in the industry do not result in rigidities and stagnation in urban economies. It is possible that developing an infrastructure geared to tourism may cause reduced resources to meet local needs. It is not just a matter of shortages in public funds. Priority adjustments may be made to ensure the supply of water, energy, and other needed resources to tourist facilities. "Tourism can cause dramatic alterations in the physical plans of urban areas as well as the positioning of other activities within them" (Chapter 8).

Costs are measurable in potential activities foregone, not to mention in inconvenience to local residents. If impacted urban areas house the base of the national economy the costs involved in the adjustment of national goals must also be considered. Such concerns must be taken most seriously, since they involve an industry which in many ways is beyond the control of the nations which host it. If tourism declines, impacts are immediate. The suprastructure of the industry, where it occupies urban settings, highlights the inflexibility of physical capital, since it may enjoy few immediate secondary uses.

Since mass tourism in Third World settings is clearly an urban phenomenon, its utility to potential host jurisdictions must be considered in that setting. The question to be answered is under what circumstances and to what extent can tourism be beneficial to host jurisdictions. In an urban context the issue relates to trade-offs between overall economic efficiency and the needs of the tourist industry. Obviously, tourism of the urban variety must be viewed in terms of how well it supports overall development goals.

Mass tourism in urban settings creates jobs. How beneficial that effect may be depends upon the skill level of the jobs in question, the level of remuneration, and who fills the job openings. If accessible jobs are created in sufficient numbers additional migration may be encouraged. The impacts of such population movements are destination specific, but they may be more significant in smaller and/or poorer areas. As was pointed out in Chapter 8, "In cases where urban expansion is driven by tourism and where local residents by and large are confined to menial, low paying jobs related to it and where the industry increases the dependence of the local economy on imports, a recipe for major problems may be being written."

Earlier in this volume it was suggested that the expansion of tourism in Third World locations may have causes in common with those underlying the emergence of production facilities owned by multinational firms. Tourist facilities may be emerging in the urban complexes of Third World nations to take advantage of cheaper labor and operating costs. This, of course, presumes that the locations selected can be marketed as tourist destinations. Indeed, such locations rely for their continuing success and profitability upon mass-marketing techniques. The customers for such tourist ventures may pay for their trips in lump sums, little of which may ever reach the Third World destinations in question.

The question becomes how much income and/or business is actually generated by tourists for domestic interests in host locations or, more succinctly, what impact will tourism have on host economies. Net revenue gains from tourism may not be needed as a justification. If whatever revenues accrue are sufficient to pay for improvements in infrastructure which are helpful to the host economy, tourism has made a positive impact. Unfortunately, negative impacts may occur if tourist revenues are used to expand the infrastructure to support tourism in ways which are detrimental to other domestic needs.

In large centers tourism may not reach a level where it impacts the physical structure and efficient functioning of the urban complex. It is merely an additional activity set that adds to the economic diversity of the area in question. In major Third World metropolitan areas mass tourism may be able to contribute to economic expansion through broadening the demand for domestic production. In order to maximize the potential for positive impacts in such settings, planners should be concerned with the placement of facilities and the use of local goods and services.

Chapter 8 suggested that "Positive impacts from tourism may be more difficult to generate and maintain in smaller nations and . . . in smaller urban complexes." Smaller jurisdictions are less likely to realize strong multiplier effects from tourism. Smaller urban areas can be permanently impacted by an overlay of operations geared to mass tourism.

If tourism generates negative externalities it can actually become an obstacle to orderly expansion. When it begins to interfere with economic expansion it may have exceeded optimum limits or it may be badly positioned and/or mismanaged. Planners must consider the dangers as well as the advantages of tourism and gear their nation's involvement to sensible dimensions. Host nations should be concerned with maximizing the benefits to be gained from tourism rather than with increasing the number of visitors. It may be that Third World urban areas would be best served by opting to host smaller numbers of upscale visitors. Such a policy should reduce the impact of the industry on infrastructure facilities and local services while at the same time reducing the danger of generating an oversupply of inflexible facilities.

Tourism can increase congestion in already crowded urban settings. This, of course, hurts the economic efficiency of the city and may even force the relocation of activities designed to service domestic needs. As suggested in Chapter 9, "Planners intending to encourage tourism as an engine of growth should ensure that it keeps a proper balance with the size of the country concerned so as not to overshadow local needs." Tourism should never be encouraged to the level where it becomes a cost rather than an advantage.

Urban places become obstacles to development if the rigidities which they harbor interfere with economic change and the needs of business. As seen above, tourist facilities can contribute to such problems. So can poorly planned or poorly positioned production facilities and infrastructure components generated for the singular needs of particular activities. Throughout the present volume various impediments to economic change in urban settings have been discussed. In each instance, ways in which such obstacles can be reduced through planning for flexibility have been suggested. If growth and development are to be encouraged, urban formats which house modern sector activities must enjoy ongoing attention from planners concerned with nurturing and facilitating economic change.

Difficulties with flexibility are hardly limited to very large metropolitan areas. They can occur in cities of any size and in economies not large enough to boast large urban complexes. Even in small nations problems related to urban structure and flexibility can be transmitted very quickly to the national economy. Indeed, the growth and development of smaller nations is linked irreversibly to the efficiency of their urban complexes.

In many Third World jurisdictions the principal urban complex may still be hampered by physical rigidities dating from colonial times. Such complexes have retained and, in many cases, increased their administrative functions since becoming the capitals of independent nations. This is true in Third World nations of all sizes. Smaller jurisdictions may even boast proportionately larger involvements by their labor forces in governmental activities. Because governmental agencies are normally housed in urban complexes, their expansion causes the urban areas in question to expand. Capital cities tend to develop in ways which facilitate government functions. If the same urban complexes that house government activities must be relied upon as major settings for private initiatives their ability to function in that secondary capacity must be examined on a case-by-case basis. Meshing private and public functions in one location will require planning.

Urban expansion fueled by the public sector and supported by demand for consumer services, not to mention other expanding manufacturing and service activities, will act as a draw for rival populations. Opportunities in consumer services are especially important in smaller nations. Third World nations of varying size may experience the emergence of various services which act as facilitators in their economies (McKee, 1988 and 1991a). By and large such services tend to be urban based and thus may reinforce the urban emphasis in the economies which host them.

Various facilitative services have been expanding in the international economy in step with the needs of multinational firms (McKee and Garner, 1992). In nations where such services are contributing to expansion by making manufacturing possible, they are also increasing expansionary pressures upon urban complexes, and thus, in turn, strengthening the urban emphasis. Some Third World jurisdictions have had the benefit of hosting various services to be sold to foreigners.

Internationally geared services have become especially visible in the economies of small Third World nations, where tourism and international financial services have risen to prominence. "In many cases the urban centers of small nations have adjusted to include sophisticated arrays of services geared to the global economy" (Chapter 9). In some such cases the services in question may be geared almost entirely to users abroad. Supporting such services may require a reworking of priorities in ways which downgrade other economic concerns. This can lead to a transportation and communications infrastructure geared to the services in question and may also result in structural adjustments in urban places which may impede the domestic functions of such locations. Planners can and should concern themselves with the nature, positioning, and volume of such services, with an eye to reducing possible negative externalities while at the same time encouraging potential benefits.

Smaller nations opting for involving themselves in international services may add to the array of goods, services, and skilled personnel to be imported. Such imports add more of an urban emphasis to economies which encourage them. The urban emphasis may be a small price to pay in economies where international services provide a real growth option. Since the urban impact on the national economy will be proportionally greater in smaller nations, it is especially important that those concerned with growth and development ensure the continuing efficiency of urban places.

It seems clear that urban complexes are important to the processes of growth and development in nations of all sizes. This is so because they are the settings in which modern sector activities choose to locate. In a Schumpeterian sense, they provide a climate for such activities to thrive. This being the case, it seems as though many who have been concerned with growth and development have not given sufficient attention or perhaps the right type of attention to urban environments. Much attention has been focused upon labor absorption and upon rural-to-urban migration and swelling informal sector activities. In attempting to understand the very real human problems that exist in Third World urban complexes, planners have placed too little emphasis on the structural difficulties which abound in those settings.

It is in the very nature of urban structures to immobilize resources. As economic change occurs the buildings and components of private and public infrastructure that exist may not have the flexibility to adapt well to new or emerging needs. Thus, the form of urban settings may actually stifle or retard certain activities which actually need urban settings to exist and prosper. Those concerned with economic expansion must add urban flexibility to the list of concerns that occupy them. It is hoped that the material in this volume will provide them with background, with respect to various ways in which urban flexibility is being impaired. If that is so, they may be able to move toward solutions to problems of development which flexibility may simplify.

Bibliography

Abu Amara, Yosra (1991). "Selected International Trade in Services and the Development of Small Economies: Some Evidence from the Caribbean Basin." Ph.D. dissertation, Kent State University.

Arizpe, Lourdes (1982). "Relay Migration and the Survival of the Peasant Household," in Helen I. Safa, ed., *Towards a Political Economy of Urbanization in Third World Countries*. New York: Oxford University Press, pp. 19–46.

Bahamas Handbook (1991). Nassau: Etienne Dupuch, Jr., Publications.

Balassa, Bela (1965). *Economic Development and Integration*. Mexico: Centro de estudios monetaríos latenamerícanos.

Barratt, P.J.H. (1982). *Grand Bahamas*. London: Macmillan Education.

Barry, T. et al. (1984). *The Other Side of Paradise: Foreign Control in the Caribbean*. New York: Grove Press.

Beckford, George L. (1972). *Persistent Poverty: Underdevelopment in Plantation Economies of the Third World*. London: Oxford University Press. Reprint, abbrev. Morant Bay, Jamaica: Maroon Publishing House, 1983.

——— (1983). "Structural Adjustment Policies in Developing Economies." *World Development* 10, no. 1 (January): 23–38.

Bluestone, Barry, and Bennett Harrison (1982). *The Deindustrialization of America*. New York: Basic Books.

Bocage, Ducarmel (1985). *The General Economic Theory of François Perroux*. Lanham, MD: University Press of America.

Boeke, J. H. (1953). *Economics and Economic Policy of Dual Societies*. New York: Institute of Pacific Relations.

Brutzkus, Eliezer (1975). "Centralized Versus Decentralized Patterns of Urbanization in Developing Countries: An Attempt to Elucidate a Guideline Principle." *Economic Development and Cultural Change* 23, no. 4: 633–52.

Buckley, Peter J., and Jeremy Clegg (1991). *Multinational Enterprises in Less Developed Countries*. New York: St. Martin's Press.

Butterworth, Douglas, and John K. Chance (1981). *Latin American Urbanization*. New York: Cambridge University Press.

Clinard, Marshall B. (1970). *Slums and Community Development*. New York: The Free Press.

Cohen, Stephen S., and John Zysman (1987). *Manufacturing Matters: The Myth of Post-Industrial Society*. New York: Basic Books.

Cross, Malcolm (1979). *Urbanization and Urban Growth in the Caribbean*. London: Cambridge University Press.

De Albuquerque, Klaus et al. (1980). "Uncontrolled Urbanization in the Developing World: A Jamaican Case Study." *Journal of Developing Areas* 14, no. 3: 361–86.

Demas, William G. (1988). "Perspectives on the Future of the Caribbean in the World Economy." *Caribbean Affairs* 1, no. 4: 6–26.

Dixon, John, Richard Carpenter, Louis Fallon, Paul Sherman, and Suparhit Manipomoke (1988). *Economic Analysis of the Environmental Impacts of Development Projects*. London: Earthskan Publications.

Doran, Michael E., and Renée A. Landes (1980). "Origin and Persistence of an Inner City Slum in Nassau." *Geographical Review* 70, no. 2: 182–93.

The Economist (2/15/92). "Pollution and the Poor," pp. 18–19.

Erbes, Robert (1973). *International Tourism and the Economy of Developing Countries*. Paris: Organization for Economic Cooperation and Development.

Fairbairn, T.I.J. (1985). *Island Economies: Studies from the South Pacific*. Suva: Institute of Pacific Studies, University of the South Pacific.

Fairbairn, Te'o I. J., and Thomas T.G. Parry (1986). *Multinational Enterprises in the Developing South Pacific Region*. Honolulu: Pacific Islands Development Program, East-West Center.

Fei, J.C.H., and Gustav Ranis (1964). *Development of the Labor Surplus Economy: Theory and Policy*. Homewood, IL: Richard D. Brown, Inc.

———— (1966). "Agrarianism, Dualism and Economic Development," in Irma Adelman and Erik Thorbeck, eds., *The Theory and Design of*

Economic Development. Baltimore: Johns Hopkins University Press, pp. 1–40.

Feketekuty, Geza (1988). *International Trade in Services.* Cambridge, MA: American Enterprise Institute/Ballinger.

Finney, Ben R., and Karen A. Watson (1977). *A New Kind of Sugar: Tourism in the South Pacific.* Honolulu: East-West Center.

Foster, Douglas (1985). *Travel and Tourism Management.* London: Macmillan Education Limited.

Frank, Andre Gunder (1967). *Capitalism and Underdevelopment in Latin America.* New York: Monthly Review Press.

——— (1979). *Dependent Accumulation and Underdevelopment.* New York: Monthly Review Press.

Frankenoff, C. A. (1967). "Elements of an Economic Model for Slums in a Developing Economy." *Economic Development and Cultural Change* 16, no. 1: 27–36.

Ghali, Moheb, ed. (1977). *Tourism and Regional Growth: An Empirical Study of the Alternative Growth Paths for Hawaii.* Leuden: Martinus Nyhoff.

Gilbert, Alan, and Josef Gugler (1981). *Cities, Poverty and Development: Urbanization in the Third World.* New York: Oxford University Press.

Hansen, Niles M. (1968). *French Regional Planning.* Bloomington: Indiana University Press.

Helleiner, G. K. (1973). "Manufacturing Exports from Less Developed Countries and Multinational Firms." *The Economic Journal* 83, no. 329: 21–47.

Henderson, J. Vernon (1988). *Urban Development: Theory, Fact and Illusion.* New York: Oxford University Press.

Herrick, Bruce, and Barclay Hudson (1981). *Urban Poverty and Economic Development.* New York: St. Martin's Press.

Higgins, Benjamin (1983). "From Growth Poles to Systems of Interactions in Space." *Growth and Change* 14, no. 4: 2–13.

Higgins, M. J. (1971). "The Internal Stratification of a Mexican Colony." *Journal of the Steward Anthropological Society* 3: 19–38.

Hirschman, Albert O. (1958). *The Strategy of Economic Development.* New Haven: Yale University Press.

Holloway, Christopher J. (1986). *The Business of Tourism.* London: Pitman Publishing, Limited.

Hope, Ronald Kemp (1986a). *Economic Development in the Caribbean.* New York: Praeger.

——— (1986b). *Urbanization in the Commonwealth Caribbean.* Boulder, CO: Westview Press.

Howard, Ebeneezer (1946). *Garden Cities of Tomorrow: A Peaceful Path to Real Reform*. London: Faber and Faber, Ltd.

Hozelitz, Bert F. (1960). *Sociological Aspects of Economic Growth*. Glencoe, IL: The Free Press.

Hudson, Brian J. (1980). "Urbanization and Planning in the West Indies." *Caribbean Quarterly* 26, no. 3: 1–17.

Innis, H. A. (1954). *The Cod Fisheries: The History of an International Economy*. 2d ed. Toronto: University of Toronto Press.

_____ (1956). *The Fur Trade in Canada: An Introduction to Canadian Economic History*. 2d ed. Toronto: University of Toronto Press.

Kannappan, Subiah (1983). *Employment Problems and the Urban Labor Market in Developing Nations*. Ann Arbor: University of Michigan.

Katzman, Martin T. (1977). *Cities and Frontiers in Brazil*. Cambridge, MA: Harvard University Press.

Khan, Habibullah, Chou Fee Seng, and Wong Kwei Cheong (1988). "The Economic and Social Impact of Tourism on Singapore," in C. A. Tisdell, C. J. Aislabie, and P. J. Stanton, eds., *Economics of Tourism: Case Study and Analysis*. Newcastle, New South Wales: Institute of Industrial Economics, University of Newcastle.

Laguerre, Michel S. (1990). *Urban Poverty in the Caribbean*. New York: St. Martin's Press.

Levy, John M. (1981). *Economic Development Programs for Cities, Counties, and Towns*. New York: Praeger.

Lewis, W. Arthur (1954). "Economic Development with Unlimited Supplies of Labor." *Manchester School* 22 (May): 139–91.

_____ (1980). "The Slowing Down of the Engine of Growth." *American Economic Review* 70, no. 4 (September): 554–64.

Linn, Johannes F. (1983). *Cities in the Developing World: Policies for Their Equitable and Efficient Growth*. New York: Oxford University Press (for the World Bank).

Lipton, M. (1975). "Urban Bias and Food Policy in Poor Countries." *Food Policy* 1: 41–52.

_____ (1977). *Why Poor People Stay Poor, A Study of Urban Bias in World Development*. London: Temple Smith.

Lowe, Marcia D. (1992). "Shaping Cities," in Lester R. Brown et al., eds., *State of the World*. New York: W. W. Norton & Company, pp. 119–37.

MacNaught, Timothy J. (1982). "Mass Tourism and the Dilemmas of Modernization in Pacific Island Communities." *Annals of Tourism Research* 9: 359–81.

Mamoozadeh, A., and D. McKee (1990). "Development through Tourism." *Tijdschrift voor economie en management* XXXV, no. 2: 147–57.

McKee, David L. (1970). "Some Economic Perversities in Metropolitan Expansion Patterns." *Nebraska Journal of Economics and Business* 9, no. 2: 53–58.

_____ (1974). "Some Reflections on Urban Dualism in Mature Economies." *The Review of Regional Studies* 4, no. 2 (Fall): 74–78.

_____ (1975). "Transportes, Urbanizacion a Integracion Economica." *Alta Direccion* XV, no. 63 (septembre–octobre): 545–50.

_____ (1977). "Facteurs exterieurs et infrastructure des pays en voie de developpement." *Revue Tiers-Monde* XVIII, no. 70 (avril–juin): 293–300.

_____ (1978). "Some Reflections on Urban Dualism in Mature Economies." *The Review of Regional Studies* 4, no. 2: 74–78.

_____ (1982). "Maín-d'oeuvre excedentaire et bidonvilles autour des metropoles du tiers-monde." *Revue Tiers-Monde* XXIII, no. 91 (juillet–septembre): 499–506.

_____ (1985). "Problemes posés par l'absorption des petites villes dans les zones urbaines des metropoles du tiers-monde." *Revue Tiers-Monde* XXVI, no. 104 (octobre–decembre): 841–47.

_____ (1986). "Tourism as a Factor in the Planning of Third World Infrastructures." *Foreign Trade Review* (July–September): 150–56.

_____ (1988). *Growth, Development, and the Rising Importance of the Service Economy in the Third World*. New York: Praeger.

_____ (1991a). *Schumpeter and the Political Economy of Change*. New York: Praeger.

_____, ed. (1991b). *Energy, the Environment and Public Policy*. New York: Praeger.

McKee, David L., and Don E. Garner (1992). *Accounting Services, The International Economy, and Third World Development*. Westport, CT: Praeger.

McKee, David L., and William H. Leahy (1970a). "Urbanization, Dualism, and Disparities in Regional Economic Development." *Land Economies* XLVI, no. 1 (February): 82–85.

_____ (1970b). "Intra-Urban Dualism in Developing Economies." *Land Economics* no. 4 (November): 486–89.

_____ (1974). "Le dualisme et l'intégration régional et urbaine." *Revue Tiers-Monde* XV, no. 58 (avril–juin): 315–25.

McKee, David L., and Gerald H. Smith (1972). "Environmental Diseconomies in Suburban Expansion." *The American Journal of Economics and Sociology* no. 2: 181–88.

McKee, David L., and Clem Tisdell (1990). *Developmental Issues in Small Island Economies*. New York: Praeger.

McLuhan, Marshall (1964). *Understanding Media: The Extensions of Man*. New York: McGraw-Hill.

McLuhan, Marshall, and Quentin Fiore (1967). *The Medium is the Message*. New York: Bantam Books, Inc.

Meller, Norman (1987). "The Pacific Island Microstates." *Journal of International Affairs* 41, no. 1 (Summer–Fall): 109–34.

Mohan, Rakesh (1979). *Urban Economic and Planning Models*. Baltimore: Johns Hopkins University Press.

Myrdal, Gunnar (1957). *Economic Theory and Underdeveloped Regions*. London: Duckworth.

North, Douglass C. (1970). "Location Theory and Regional Economic Growth," reprinted in David L. McKee et al., eds., *Regional Economics: Theory and Practice*. New York: The Free Press, pp. 29–48.

Noyelle, Thierry J., and Thomas M. Stanback, Jr. (1984). *The Economic Transformation of American Cities*, Totowa, NJ: Rowman & Allanheld Publishers.

Noyelle, Thierry J., and Anna B. Dutka (1988). *International Trade in Business Services*. Cambridge, MA: Ballinger.

Nurkse, Ragnar (1967). *Problems of Capital Formation in Underdeveloped Countries and Patterns of Trade and Development*. New York: Oxford University Press.

Paelinck, Jean (1965). "La théorie du développement régional polarisé." *Cahiers de l'Institute de Science Economique Appliques*, Series L, no. 15 (March).

Palmer, Ransford W. (1979). *Caribbean Dependence on the United States Economy*. New York: Praeger.

_____ (1984). *Problems of Development in Beautiful Countries: Perspectives on the Caribbean*. Lanham, MD: The North-South Publishing Co.

Parry, Thomas G. (1973). "The International Firm and National Economic Policy." *The Economic Journal* 84, no. 332: 1201–21.

Pearson, Charles S., ed. (1987). *Multinational Corporations, Environment and the Third World*. Durham: Duke University Press.

Perroux, F. (1950). "Economic Space: Theory and Applications." *Quarterly Journal of Economics* 64, no. 1 (February): 89–104.

_____ (1964). *L'Economie du XXe Siècle*. 2d ed., enl. Paris: Presse Universitaire de Paris.

_____ (1970). "Note on the Concept of Growth Poles," in David L. McKee, Robert D. Dean, and William H. Leahy, eds., *Regional Economics: Theory and Practice*. New York: The Free Press, pp. 93–104.

_____ (1988). "The Pole of Development's New Place in a General Theory of Economic Activity," in Benjamin Higgins and Donald J. Savoie, *Regional Economic Development*. Boston: Unwin Hyman, pp. 48–76.

Ponting, Clive (1991). *A Green History of the World*, New York: St. Martin's Press.

Portes, Alejandro, and Lauren Benton (1984). "Industrial Development and Labor Absorption: A Reinterpretation." *Population and Development Review* no. 4 (December): 589–613.

Ratcliff, Richard V. (1949). *Urban Land Economics*. New York: McGraw-Hill Book Co., Inc.

Reich, Robert B. (1992). *The Work of Nations*. New York: Vintage Books.

Roberts, Bryan (1978). *Cities of Peasants*. Beverly Hills: Sage Publications.

Rodwin, Lloyd (1970). *Nations and Cities*. Boston: Houghton Mifflin Company.

Rothblatt, Donald N. (1974). *National Policy for Urban and Regional Development*. Lexington, MA: D.C. Heath and Company.

Safa, Helen I. (1982). *Towards a Political Economy of Urbanization in Third World Countries*. Delhi: Oxford University Press.

Santos, Milton (1979). *The Shared Space: The Two Circuits of the Urban Economy in Underdeveloped Countries*. New York: Methuen.

Schmidheiny, Stephen (1992). *Changing Course: A Global Business Perspective on Development and the Environment*. Cambridge, MA: Business Council for Sustainable Development/MIT Press.

Schramm, Gunter, and Jeremy J. Warford, eds. (1989). *Environmental Management and Economic Development*. Baltimore: Johns Hopkins University Press.

Segal, A., ed. (1975). *Population Policies in the Caribbean*. Lexington, MA: D. C. Heath and Co.

Stanback, Thomas M., Jr., Peter J. Bearce, Thierry J. Noyelle, and Robert A. Karasek (1981). *Services: The New Economy*. Totowa, NJ: Allanheld, Osman & Co. Publishers, Inc.

Stanback, Thomas M., Jr., and Thierry J. Noyelle (1982). *Cities in Transition*. Totowa, NJ: Allanheld & Osman Publishers.

Stokes, Charles J. (1962). "A Theory of Slums." *Land Economics* XXXVIII, no. 3: 187–97.

Sundquist, James L. (1970). "A Policy for Urban Growth I: Where Shall They Live?" *The Public Interest*, no. 18 (Winter) 1970: 88–100.

Thomas, Vinod (1985). "Evaluating Pollution Control: The Case of Sao Paulo, Brazil." *Journal of Development Economics* 19: 133–46.

Thompson, Anthony (1979). *An Economic History of the Bahamas*. Nassau: Commonwealth Publications, Limited.

Tisdell, C. (1975). "The Theory of Optimal City-Sizes: Elementary Speculation about Analysis and Policy." *Urban Studies* 12: 61–70.

——— (1987). "Tourism, the Environment and Profit." *Economic Analysis & Policy* 17, no. 1: 13–30.

——— (1990). *Natural Resources, Growth and Development.* New York: Praeger.

Tisdell, C., C. J. Aislabie, and P. J. Stanton, eds. (1988). *Economics of Tourism: Case Study and Analysis.* Newcastle, New South Wales: Institute of Industrial Economics, University of Newcastle.

Todaro, M. P. (1971). "Income Expectations, Rural-Urban Migration and Employment in Africa." *International Labor Review* (November): 387–413.

Todaro, Michael P. (1969). "A Model of Labor Migration and Urban Unemployment in Less Developed Countries." *American Economic Review* 59, no. 1: 138–48.

——— (1989). *Economic Development in the Third World.* 4th ed. New York: Longman.

Tucker, Ken, and Mark Sundberg (1988). *International Trade in Services.* London: Routledge.

United Nations (1990). *World Urbanization Prospects.* New York, United Nations.

United Nations (1991). *Human Development Report 1991.* New York: Oxford University Press.

United Nations Centre for Human Settlements (1981). *The Residential Circumstances of the Urban Poor in Developing Countries.* New York: Praeger.

Walker, Bruce (1981). *Welfare Economics and Urban Problems.* New York: St. Martin's Press.

Wilsher, Peter, and Rosemary Righter (1975). *The Exploding Cities.* New York: Quadrangle Books.

World Bank (1992). *World Development Report 1992: Development and the Environment.* New York: Oxford University Press.

World Commission on Environment and Development (1987). *Our Common Future.* New York: Oxford University Press.

Worrell, DeLisle (1987). *Small Island Economies: Structure and Performance in the English-Speaking Caribbean Since 1970.* New York: Praeger.

Wright, Frank Lloyd (1958). *The Living City.* New York: Horizon Press.

Yepes, Guellermo (1990). *Management and Operational Practices of Municipal and Regional Water and Sewerage Companies in Latin America and the Caribbean,* Report INU-61. Washington, DC: World Bank, Infrastructures and Urban Development Department.

Index

Amazon Region, 21
Arizpe, Lourdes, 40
Asian Tigers, 96

Bahamas, 21, 110, 112
balance of payments, 96, 122
barrios, 67
Brasilia, 21
Brazil, 20

Caribbean Basin region, 112, 113, 114, 118, 121, 122, 124
Central America, 18, 39
central business district (CBD), 6–7, 69, 114, 134

deindustrialization, 15, 25
Demas,William S., 126
dualism: based on exports, 95–96; blockage of growth and, 35, 142; economic dualism, 32, 95, 142; impact on developmental infrastructures, 158; impact on economic integration, 88, 94, 158; manufacturing activities and, 96, 97; negative externalities of, 34, 158; social dualism, 95; urban labor markets and, 34, 143; urban settings and, 29, 35, 36, 143; as a stage in development, 94

environmental damage, 73
environmental diseconomies, 76

Feketekuty, Geza, 123
Frankenoff, C. A., 48–49
Freeport/Lucaya area (Grand Bahamas), 22

global economy, 103, 126, 157
Grand Bahamas, 21–22
growth poles, 20, 24, 27, 139

Haiti, 39

import substitution, 24, 88, 93–94, 96–97, 100, 122–123, 129

informal sector: as a halfway
    house, 49; impact on workers,
    37; migration decisions and,
    66, 166; neoclassical labor ab-
    sorption models and, 55; in
    smaller nations, 121; squatter
    settlements and, 48, 66, 149;
    urban settings for, 37, 55, 59;
    welfare expectations and, 55,
    56, 149
Innis, Harold, 91
international economy, 25

Jamaica, 93, 107

Katzman, Martin, 76–77, 78, 153

labor absorption, 28, 32, 33, 34, 38
Latin America, 20, 21, 52, 118
Lewis, W. Arthur, 23, 26, 35, 38
London, 20
Los Angeles, 63, 68
Lowe, Marcia, 73, 77–78

market mechanism, 3
McLuhan, Marshall, 12
Mexico, 38, 40; Mexico City, 52,
    53, 82, 84, 110
multinational corporations
    (firms): environmental prob-
    lems and, 82, 156; facilitative
    services and, 125–126, 165; im-
    pact upon infrastructures, 98,
    100; low labor costs, 97, 162–
    163; positioning of facilities,
    82, 98, 160; as power centers,
    99; Third World settings and,
    24, 82, 90, 98, 140; in tourism,
    105–106, 109, 113; uncertain-
    ties from, 84, 99
multinucleated metropolitan ar-
    eas, 64, 68–69, 71
Myrdal, Gunnar, 30, 31

natural environment, 73
Naussau (Bahamas), 22, 110, 112–
    113
negative externalities, 38, 114,
    134, 144, 155–156
New Providence (Bahamas), 112,
    114
North, Douglass, 91
Noyelle, Thierry J., 13–15, 136–
    137

Orinoco River, 21

Paelinck, Jean, 99
Palmer, Ransford, 108
Paris, 20
Perroux, François, 23, 98
pole theory, 33, 139
pollution, 73, 74, 76, 82–84
Port of Spain (Trinidad), 51
primary exports, 89, 95, 122

Reich, Robert, 109
rigidities: declining tourism and,
    161; as impediments to
    change, 12, 164; metropolitan
    infrastructures as, 134; as ob-
    stacles to development, 164;
    resulting from primary pro-
    duction for export, 158; in
    small economies, 165; in ur-
    ban structure, 5, 13, 29, 30,
    134, 164
Roberts, Bryan, 36, 37, 143

San Juan, 67, 68, 116
Schumpeter, Joseph, 23, 30, 166
secondary economic pursuits, 8
service activities, 6, 134
services: ascendancy of, 13; avail-
    ability through rural/urban
    integration, 40; for export,
    126, 127; as facilitators, 124–

126, 165; impact in small economies, 120, 126, 129; international scope of, 103; in metropolitan environments, 14, 57, 65, 69, 134, 155

slums: absorptive capacity of, 47, 62; in advanced economies, 46, 51; benefits from infrastructure, 47; elimination of, 50, 51, 53; function of, 50; as impediments to urban expansion, 47, 52, 63, 148; necessary and unnecessary, 51, 52, 148; as part of growth processes, 48, 49, 149; planned positioning of, 53, 56, 148; safety in, 53; squatter settlements as, 46; subminimal standards in, 47; surplus labor and, 46, 145; in Third World metropolitan areas, 46, 49, 51, 52, 146; in Third World nations, 51

spread effects, 7

squatters: environmental difficulties and, 76–78; as a fait accompli, 48; natural disasters and, 52; positioning of, 52, 69, 80, 130; provision of space for, 149; reasons for in migration, 51; removal of, 50, 51, 56, 58, 150; retarding growth in, 51; self-improvement programs of, 53; universal in Third World metropolitan areas, 45, 51; urban services and, 53, 104, 148

squatter settlements: burgeoning populations in, 54; economic self-interest of residents, 51, 52, 149; environmental concerns and, 58, 78–82, 149, 156; extending public services to, 47, 48, 53, 57, 79–81, 110–111,

146; functions of, 46, 50; heterogeneity of population, 51; improvements in, 51, 52, 53, 79, 148, 149; interferences with expanding infrastructures, 47, 57, 66, 70, 146, 149; metropolitan expansion and, 47, 57, 63, 66, 149; migration to, 54, 79, 147, 155; modern sector pursuits and, 49, 146; overproliferation of, 52, 54, 147; as planning concepts, 50, 54, 56, 82, 147; positioning of, 46, 52, 56, 59, 63, 66, 81, 110, 130; positive role for, 48–49, 146, 147; removal of, 50, 51, 56, 58, 147, 149; unpredictability of, 52, 77, 146, 147; urban expansion and, 47, 57, 63, 66, 148; urban survival options and, 48

Stanback, Thomas M., Jr., 13–15, 136, 137

staple commodities (staples): development and, 90–91, 94, 156; effects of depletion, 92; export of, 91–94, 156; infrastructure and, 92, 95, 158; need for in advanced nations, 90–92; North American development and, 92; terms of trade and, 91, 93, 156

structural rigidities, 4, 9

Summers, Lawrence, 83, 84

surplus labor: absorption into the modern sector, 38, 143; in agriculture, 39; educational needs, 121; movement into metropolitan areas, 23, 38, 39, 46, 66; in multinucleated metropolitan areas, 69, 153; proliferation of slums and, 45, 145; service requirements, 48, 146; undesirability in urban settings, 123

tertiary economic pursuits, 8
Third World: altering locations
of capitals in, 21; directing
metropolitan expansion in, 67;
domestic markets in smaller
jurisdictions in, 27; dualism
in, 94, 158; export services in,
126–127; external impacts on
infrastructures in, 98, 100; labor absorption and growth in,
34–35; lack of urban planning
in, 69; macroeconomic issues,
19, 23, 35, 41; manufacturing
in, 18, 27, 80, 100; metropolitan viability in, 22; multinational firms in, 80, 96, 160;
need for urban planning in,
33, 67, 70; pollution in, 82–84;
population growth in cities of,
26, 38, 39, 61, 68, 142; rural/ur-
ban employment adjustments
in, 39, 62, 66, 144; squatter settlements in, 49, 51, 58, 66, 77,
81, 130; staple exports from,
91; surplus labor in, 33, 66;
tourism in, 104, 107, 109, 114–
115, 160–161; urban bias and,
62; urban efficiency in, 24, 28;
urban employment expecta-
tions in, 59, 66, 121, 145; urban
environmental problems in,
73–75, 77, 82, 130; urban flexibility in, 17, 25, 26, 28, 31, 32–
34, 134, 137, 139, 183; urban
poor in, 46, 80; urban positioning and development in, 19;
urban rigidities in, 118, 134,
136
Third World economies: absorption of peripheral settlements,
66, 67; decline in rural profit
opportunities in, 40; environmental difficulties in, 75, 82;

export activities in, 27, 100;
foreign linkages, 24, 89–90,
100, 103; land fragmentation
in, 39; leading sectors of, 145;
macro role of cities in, 28, 45;
manufacturing facilities in, 18,
24, 25, 82, 140; modern sector
activities in, 22, 23, 137, 138,
140, 141; multinucleated urban areas in, 64, 66, 67, 69;
need for urban planning in,
67, 142; pollution in, 82, 83; positioning of urban complexes,
18; sustainable development
in, 26; tourism, 104, 106, 160,
161; urban slums in, 52
Third World metropolitan complexes: absorption of urban
places, 63, 64, 67, 151; crisis response planning, 72; eco-
nomic expansion and, 31, 33,
41, 138; efficient expansion of,
35, 38, 47, 67, 146; environmental difficulties, 75, 76–77,
82, 84–85, 154, 156; flexibility,
17, 31, 166; informal sector employment, 55, 66, 69; labor absorption in, 34–35, 55;
multinucleated, 63, 64, 66, 67,
68, 69, 72, 153; national development and, 45, 115, 138, 145;
over expansion of, 36, 66;
squatter settlements in, 47, 51,
54, 69, 77, 81, 146, 147; surplus
labor, 23, 26, 124, 144; tourism
in, 104, 105, 107, 110, 111, 115,
160, 163
Third World nations: environmental difficulties, 77, 82, 85;
governmental bureaucracies,
119; impacts of business activities, 26–27; interferences with
development aims of, 25; lead-

ing economic sectors of, 17; manufacturing for export, 100, 123; multinational firms and, 82, 97, 140; primary exports, 91, 157, 165; service exports, 126, 157, 165; services as facilitators in, 123, 124, 126, 165; slums and, 46, 146; small nations, 100, 128, 165–166; tourism and, 104, 106, 114, 161, 164, 210; urban agglomerations in, 31, 144; urban expansion in, 63, 64, 119; urban structural rigidities, 118–119, 136, 141

Tisdell, C. A., 33, 34, 49, 74, 75, 76, 154

tourism: advanced nations and, 103, 160; contributor to development, 104, 105, 115, 163, 164; government revenues and, 110; local impacts of, 104, 106, 107, 114; local service benefits, 110, 115; mass tourism, 105, 107–111, 113, 161, 162; negative externalities, 110, 112, 128, 163, 164; net revenue gains from, 110; positive impacts from, 104, 110–114, 128, 163; public

expenditures and, 110; public service needs, 161; risks from, 105, 112, 113, 114, 161–162, 164; urban expansion through, 109, 115, 162; urban settings for, 103, 104, 105, 106, 108, 110, 115

United States, 4, 8, 13, 25, 63, 68, 74, 103, 104, 133
urban bias, 19, 27, 29–30, 41, 62, 94, 97, 143
urban flexibility, 17, 132
urbanization: concentration of activity from, 29; economic development and, 30–31, 141; environmental concerns, 30, 73–75, 154; growth of larger centers, 61; in small economies, 117; in wealthier nations, 63; macro implications of, 19
urban services, 65
urban service sector, 6
urban sprawl, 8

Venezuela, 21

World Bank, 83
Wright, Frank Lloyd, 5
Worrell, DeLisle, 125

About the Author

DAVID L. McKEE is Professor of Economics at Kent State University. He is a specialist in economic development and regional economics, and his research has been widely published in professional journals in the United States and abroad. His recent books include *Schumpeter and the Political Economy of Change*; *Growth, Development, and the Service Economy in the Third World*; *Developmental Issues in Small Island Economies* (coauthored with Clement Tisdell), and *Accounting Services, the International Economy and Third World Development* (coauthored with Don E. Garner).